WHAT PEOPLE HAVE TO SAY ABOUT

THE REMARKABLE MAN

"The old model of what it means to be a man is outdated and about as useful as a cassette tape for your MP3 player.

The idea that men can run off to some self made cave and disengage just creates greater challenges. Men end up feeling isolated from each other, women don't feel that they can emotional trust these men, and children grow up believing men are incapable of emotional depth. In this Book Dwayne does a brilliant job of bringing to light a new model for men. The result is that Men around the world are coming together and are hearing the call for connection and for a brotherhood they can believe in and trust. Dwayne's book is of great service to Men, Women and Children. I believe men have been waiting for a way to embrace all of who they are so as to become and Dwayne Klassen gives it to then in the form of: The Remarkable Man."

– Dov Baron, Bestselling Author, Authentic Leadership Mentor and the world's only Corporate Cultural Momentum Strategist. President, Baron Mastery Institute.

"Men, read this book as if your life depended upon it. This book lays out a challenge before all men to fulfill their true purpose and to be authentically masculine while stepping up and becoming Remarkable Men."

– Darren Jacklin, Professional Speaker, Corporate Trainer, Business Coach & Best Selling Author

"Dwayne has built a bridge for men to re-connect and embrace their Authentic Masculine Energy. Gentlemen if you want to move from ordinary to REMAKABLE this is a must read. Ladies, if you want to better understand men, this is it."

— **Franco Lombardo, Cofounder Veritage, Speaker and Author of:** *Great White Elephant, Why Rich Kids Hate Their Parents!,* **and** *Money Motto, The Path to Authentic Wealth*

THE
REMARKABLE
MAN

Champions to Women
Heroes to Children
Brothers to Each Other

AVIVA
PUBLISHING
NEW YORK

DWAYNE H. KLASSEN

The Remarkable Man: *Champions to Women, Heroes to Children, Brothers to Each Other*

For inquiries, please contact:

Dwayne H. Klassen

www.RemarkableManProject.com

ISBN: 978-1-935586-69-2

Editor: Jeannine Malory
Proofreader: Tyler Tichelaar
Cover Design & Interior Layout: Fusion Creative Works, www.fusioncw.com

First Edition

For additional copies visit: www.RemarkableManProject.com

ACKNOWLEDGMENTS

This book symbolizes my "Everest"—the biggest challenge and personal ascent of my life. However, without the work, faith, and encouragement of my family, friends, and brothers of The Remarkable Man Project, this quest wouldn't have come to completion. Thank you for being in my life when it mattered most.

To my sister, Karen: Thank you for knowing that I was to be an agent of change for men. Your belief in me when I had little for myself has been, and always will be, a source of strength and inspiration for me. I honor your journey and am proud and humbled to be your brother. You are bold, beautiful, and brilliant in more ways than I could express here. We are souls riding the lightning together!

To my mom, Lorraine, and my dad, Henry: You're my biggest fans, parents who give more unconditional love and support than anyone could imagine. Mom, you gave me shelter when I had none, food when I was hungry, and encouragement and light during my darkest days. Dad, you're my best friend and hero. You embody what a Remarkable Man is to me. You wear your heart on your sleeve and are an example any son would be proud to follow. I take comfort in knowing you have my back. You're the best, Dad!

To Laura Simonson: You are one of the most amazing, giving, and unselfish people I have ever met. Your support, guidance, and friendship helped create The Remarkable Man brand as it is today. Thank you for your monumental encouragement and feedback during this journey.

To my Remarkable Men: You are my brothers, the pioneers, early adopters, and vision-keepers who saw the possibilities in this journey and took that first step to become founding members. I salute you as the Remarkable Men you are.

To Murray Ellix, the first Remarkable Man project member: We've gone down an interesting road over the years, my friend. You put your faith in me many times and I honor you for that. Cheers, mate!

To J.B King, Dan Giercke, Alexander Jamieson, Tym Sotnikow, Oleg Kuzmin, Cory Maystrowich, David Martin, Jay Fiset, Steve Nunuk, Lee Ellis, Thomas Fabbri, Franco Lombardo, Randy Lennon and Don Lajoie: You were there at the start and stayed through the greatest growing pains. You provided support and encouragement every step of the way. You saw what was there long before it came to fruition. Thank you for having my back.

To Dov Baron: You have the most powerful form of "Kung-Fu" for life mastery I have ever experienced. A true Remarkable man! The world needs your sage and wisdom. I honor the path you are on my friend.

To the rest of the Remarkable Man Project Tribe: Darren Jacklin, Todd Purcell, Bill Drake, Abe Dueck, Rafael Talavera, Paul Puzanoski, Charles Bae, Carter Nagel and Robert Hubbs: I honor your commitment to be Remarkable in all you are. Thank you, my brothers.

To Patrick Snow: Thank you for your guidance. I'm grateful to you for giving me the kick in the pants I needed to complete this book, as well as for introducing me to Jeannine Mallory and Tyler Tichelaar:

High praise to you both for your talent, and expertise for putting my words into a cohesive and legible piece of literature. Well done!

To Shiloh Schroeder: Thank you for your patience and helping to bring my dream to life. Your talents that brought this book into physical form are greatly appreciated.

CONTENTS

INTRODUCTION

You are what you are and where you are because of
what has gone into your mind.
You can change what you are and where you are
by changing what goes into your mind.
— Zig Ziglar

The information in this book will be of great value to both men and women. A Remarkable Man's energy can take relationships to a new level of understanding and appreciation. Through this book, men will learn to empower themselves and become more confident, charismatic, and fully aware of where they're going. What this book brings to your relationships (both intimate and platonic) will alter your perception of true bliss and happiness.

As much as this book is directed toward men, I believe women will read it too. There's something intriguing, attractive, and inspiring about a Remarkable Man. When a woman finds a Remarkable Man, she will notice, appreciate, and honor who and what he is.

Gentlemen, it has never been more imperative to find the authentic, masculine man within you. What do I mean by "authentic, masculine man"? Throughout time, men have lived and acted based on an egotistical masculine energy. From this place, we have waged wars, beat our chests, and stomped our feet to get what we wanted or needed. However, as we evolve, we're becoming more *authentic*, masculine men. We're becoming men who understand who and what we are, and what we're capable of doing. We're becoming men who live unapologetically, from a masculine, heart-centered, place within our souls. This is the life of The Remarkable Man.

NOW is the time for The Remarkable Man to emerge in society. We have many reasons to be thankful and happy. Yet few of us actually live that way. What prevents *you* from living the life you know you can live, the life you know you *want* to live, the life you are meant to live?

Throughout the ages, one truth has governed how we live. This truth can change our experiences in moments. We can shift from victim to victor. We can change doubt to inspiration, and we can go from being in debt and despair to enjoying wealth, joy, and abundance. You'll find this truth within these pages.

How many times have you read an inspiring book that seemed to have all the answers? You read it thoroughly, maybe twice, perhaps took notes, or kept track of the lessons taught in its pages. You felt a personal shift and said something like, "My life is going to get better now! I'm a changed person. I'll never look back. Look out world; here I come!" Sound familiar? If you've gone through such an experience, then you also realize that somehow, the lessons and resulting experience don't provide the dream life you thought would come.

Crazy, isn't it? It drives you nuts when you think about how many times you've repeated the same words. I hear you, my brothers! I know exactly how you feel because I was there for a large part of my life. I've had experiences I wouldn't wish upon anyone. Back then, it was easier to blame circumstances outside myself for everything in life. And, of course, I could justify everything. *How could I be to blame for all this? It's too big. I'm a good person. I treat people right and do my best to respect everyone. A good person like me couldn't possibly cre-*

ate all this crap! But here's the truth: I created it all. To use a motion picture analogy, in the movie called *My Life*, I created everything—the actors, stagehands, camera crew, writers, promoters, investors—yes, everything!

It's not easy to admit you've created your own reality because it brings you closer to the truth (which might not be good). It takes you away from your ego, where you've been comfortable. Ego makes you struggle. Ego doesn't want you to know it's caused everything in your life. For the most part, you are where you are because of your ego.

Looking back, I realize I was far from Remarkable in most areas of my life. I can own up to it now. I enjoyed being in leadership roles, but I rarely followed through. This lack of effort caused me to live a half-lived life. I missed many experiences because I was too afraid, too damaged, too inexperienced, or too broke.

Why was I so afraid? What was I trying to avoid, no matter the cost? What scared me to such an extent that I sacrificed much of my life to avoid it? Was it fear of failure, fear of rejection, fear of the unknown, or fear of not being loved? **What was it?**

In truth, it was none of the above. I just didn't know who I was. It's weird, but I was afraid of my essence, my successful self, and the God-man in me. You see, I'd always believed I'd be successful, a dynamic force for good, a man of vision, strength, and courage—but it scared the hell out of me. To reach those places, I would have to step away from my ego and experience life in a way I couldn't imagine. I mean, it would require *hard work*, long hours, and dedication on a level that made me cringe. I'd need to deal with my ego and my "other selves," which were not serving me. In reality, I'd suffered needlessly at the hands of a self that was weak and small.

Once I recognized I had power over that weak and small self, I was free, but filled with regret at having allowed myself to live that way.

After struggling through a combination of life-altering challenges, I decided I was finished playing the victim. I vowed to start living. I was ready to uncover every aspect of my life that had thwarted my growth. This urge was strong in me, like the DNA code in a bird that tells the bird when it's time to fly south. The bird has no choice but to follow its instinct, its calling. A similar calling had been growing and gnawing at me most of my adult life, but I'd created dramas and distractions to avoid it. When you try to fight your own destiny, there's little chance you will emerge the victor. You might fool yourself for a while, but eventually, your old, familiar lessons come back around to point you in the direction you must go.

As the world around me began to change, I knew my place in it needed to get bigger. And so, I let go. I surrendered and allowed grace to flow through me. I needed to prepare myself for a larger role. I couldn't ignore or run away from my destiny; the Universe wouldn't let me do it. It was time for me to be Remarkable.

The Remarkable Man Project is the result of my journey to get where I am today, and more. The journey paved the way for me to live the life I knew I should live. No more half-life, no more suffering, no more being the victim, no more wishing and hoping. If I wanted my life to change, I had to show up in my life *and* in the lives of those I cared about. What I know today is that my life back then wasn't authentic. It wasn't about living with purpose and passion.

Has there been a defining moment in your life? Think about what occurred when you realized, "This is it! This is what I've been waiting for." Then—*BOOM!*—your life changed in that one defining moment. Does such a moment in time exist? Is it a brief but powerful insight, experience, or event? Is it a series of events ? Maybe it's all of the above. What you experience in your defining moment is *synchronicity*. In your one defining moment, you experience an event that defies everything you know about cause and effect. In that one beautiful moment, we piece it all together and say, "Aha! So *that's* what this is all about!"

Our world is shifting quickly. You can feel it. A new pattern of energy is unfolding. Men, in general terms, feel more disconnected, frustrated, and alone than at any other time in history. We're confused because we don't know how to act and interpret that which defines us. What is our role, our "utility," and our value in this place and time?

Yes, the world is shifting, and women are leading the way. Have you noticed it yet? Quietly, and in some cases not so quietly, women are celebrating their hard-earned empowerment. Women are the driving force in most households. There are more women's groups and "women-only" organizations than ever before. Women are connecting, growing, and supporting each other unlike any other time in history. In fact, because my sister, Karen, is the founder of Women Embracing Brilliance, an international women's organization, I've seen firsthand how popular these groups have become.

As for us, well...while there are many wonderful organizations for men, unless you belong to one, you probably don't know they exist. For some reason, men's groups seem to keep a low profile. Many women's groups focus on empowerment, learning, healing, and support. They run the gamut, from self-help and personal growth, to business and investing. If you do some research, you'll find there are few such groups available to men. How many men do you know who meet and support each other on a regular basis? Sadly, unless it involves a flat-screen TV and some beer, most men don't or won't connect on that level.

Guys, when you think about it, I think you'll agree that women are evolving faster than we are. Women are growing—spiritually, mentally, emotionally, and financially—more quickly than men. This situation has to change, men, and soon! Think about it. What kind of men do you think these empowered, strong, and evolving women want? They want men who do more than just keep up with them; they want men who will inspire and challenge them. Yep, they want it all! They're looking for men who "get" them on all levels. I'm not describing an "Us vs. Them" scenario. I'm not implying we have to appease women from a place of being less-than. I am very unapologetic about that. We are men and we should be proud to be men. We must have dignity, and genuine masculine power.

My point is that men are falling behind on the road to self-actualization. We need to accept this situation in order to have the kind of relationships we desire. This need is especially true if you're in a relationship with an ever-evolving woman. Trust me. When a man digs deep into the core of who he is and his mission is to understand himself, women take notice.

It's time to embrace your authentic, masculine energy for what it is. It's time to honor, accept, and understand the feminine energy in and around you. It's time to see how this energy serves you and, conversely, how it takes away your power.

This book will be a catalyst in helping you understand your place in the world. It will let you know you are not alone. The Remarkable Man is not someone else. He's not an impossible image to behold. He's not somewhere else—leaping tall buildings or performing superhuman feats. He's in you, and you know it to be true.

The Remarkable Man in you is connected to the Remarkable Man in me. We are traveling this road together. We are brothers united to make a difference and raise the status to what it means to be a man, a true twenty-first century man. In the pages ahead, you will find information that will change the way you see yourself and will empower you to find what makes you rock in all areas of your life.

This book is my destiny, a way to uplift men. My goal is to lift you to the place you want to be. This book is designed to bring out your "Big Self," your "A-Game," and the divine essence of who you are as a man.

Gentlemen, now is our time! It's time to show the world what authentic masculine men can do as harbingers of greatness. It's time to be champions to women, heroes to children, and brothers to each other. Gentlemen, it is time to be Remarkable!

PART ONE

THE STARTING POINT

CHAPTER ONE

I'VE GOT YOUR BACK!

Wherever a man turns, he can find someone who needs him.
— Albert Schweitzer

That day, I didn't dread my train trip back to the suburbs. I was buoyed by the idea that soon I'd be moving into a place in the city, where I longed to be. I'd finally inked a lease on a downtown condo that was close to work and located in a vibrant, hip neighborhood I always knew I'd get to. I wouldn't miss the daily commute at all. However, my seemingly routine trip was about to be unlike any other. It was a late Sunday afternoon and the passenger traffic was light. Only about eight of us were in the car, each of us oblivious of one another as we occupied our own little worlds. There was one man behind me, a girl in her mid-teens two seats up and across from me, a girl with red hair near the center, and an elderly Indian couple with their two grandchildren, a boy about seven years old and a girl who looked to be a year or so older. They looked tired and must have had a long day.

The Sky Train is a fully-automated elevated rapid transit system in Vancouver, one of the best in the world. It rides the rails some sixty feet above the ground so you get a great view every time. I'm one of the people who doesn't mind the trip. As we headed east, I faced away from our destination. I found myself thinking about how great life would be when I moved downtown at the end of the month.

My thoughts were interrupted while we waited briefly at the Broadway station. Just as the automated doors were about to close...the darkness stepped in.

It was as if I were seeing a scene from the movie *Terminator*. My eyes first saw the scuffed-up and noticeably large Doc Martin stompers, then up past the army-issue camouflage pants to the lone beer can dangling from a stretched-out six-pack holder. Oh, and he held a beer in his oversized, fingerless leather gloves. My eyes made it to the top of a very bald head some six feet from the floor. The doors closed behind him and the train resumed its journey east. He staggered slightly as the train lurched ahead. If he'd gone without notice when he entered, he was about to change that in a hurry. This formidable man was a skinhead, complete with jet-black tattoos on his biceps and neck, up past his ears. Most of the tattoos' words are not fit to print here, but let's just say he had plenty of Nazi praise on permanent display on his pale, white skin.

He balanced himself without grabbing the pole, took a big gulp from his beer, and looked in my direction. Then he shocked everyone in the car when he pointed to us and blurted, "Fuck you! Fuck you! And Fuck you!"

And he meant it.

With that, the alpha male had made his presence known—and he seemed pleased to wield such power. Making eye contact was not something at the top of my mind at that moment. Fear gripped me, and I felt the trip was not going to end well.

He stood near the center of the car, and he had yet to look to the other side. As he pivoted around to survey his domain, he noticed the Indian family seated almost directly behind him. With sick, gleeful exuberance, he pointed at them and slurred loudly, "Oh, no way. I can't believe this!" As he tried to restrain himself, he pumped his huge fists in the air, spilling what was left of his beer. "*You* people...."

I will not repeat the angry, hateful words he directed toward the Indian family. What I heard and saw was painful and utterly disgusting. The children were petrified, and the elderly couple was overcome with terror.

"Hey, old man, it's time for you to die," he snarled. "Me and you are going to have a little fun." With that, he punched an advertising sign above the man's turban with such force that the bang startled everyone in the car. I could tell he wasn't going to back down. He actually wanted to hurt the grandfather, and it looked like it was going to happen soon.

I was filled with both angst and helplessness. No one was doing anything; no one could. Someone needed to do something, or we were going to witness a beating. I'm not a violent man. Up to that moment, I'd been in two fights. One was an epic failure, and the other was a life-changing win. That day on the Sky Train, I felt sick, scared, and torn.

There are times in life when good judgment and rational thinking go out the window for reasons we don't understand, and, rational thinking be damned...it was about to happen to me.

"That's not going to happen!" I blurted.

What the hell am I doing? Where did that come from? It was too late for me to suck the words back into my mouth. And with that, I'd just challenged an enraged, inebriated, racist. He outweighed me by at least forty pounds, and I assumed he ate people like me for lunch. My heart was pounding out of my chest!

Upon hearing my words, he reacted like a Tyrannosaurus Rex that's just heard a branch break behind it. He became alert to the sound, and pivoted around with an evil look of satisfaction to confirm what he'd just heard. "Who said that?" he bellowed as he looked at me, knowing it was me. He pointed to me, and there was contempt and fury in his voice as he said, "Oh, man, I'm gonna bust up Gramps (he didn't use that word); then I'm gonna bust up *you*!"

The train stopped at another station, but there weren't any riders for our car. Oddly, none of the passengers budged to escape. It was an unusual pause, like a commercial break, as everyone waited for the doors to close.

As the doors slid shut, I found myself blurting, "No! You're gonna leave them alone. At the next station, it's just gonna be you and me!"

Dwayne, shut the hell up! What are you doing? My mind was racing.

With that, he swung toward me, using the grab bar above the couple. He seemed to have his own monkey bars as he kicked his legs out hard and jumped to the car floor with a hard thud. "Oh, I'm gonna love watching you bleed," he snarled.

I was seized with dread and couldn't imagine a more foolish act of bravery. Then, as I pondered my doom, something amazing took place. I felt a hand on my shoulder, and then a man's voice uttered the most wonderful and empowering words I could have heard at that fateful moment. Just behind my ear, I heard the man's low, reassuring voice. **"I've got your back,"** he said.

Without turning to acknowledge this godsend, I nodded slightly to let him know I'd heard him.

What those four words did was nothing short of miraculous. I felt solidarity, connection, and had hope of getting out alive. I was not alone! A brother I didn't even know had stepped up in a dangerous situation to help right a wrong. As these feelings moved through me, I suddenly had some clarity of thought. I remembered a friend of mine was part of some beta testing for the Sky Train line. He'd told me that each car was equipped with microphones so security could hear what was happening in the train. "Good God," I thought. "I hope he was right because I'm gambling with my life here."

I mustered up all the bravado I could find, and said to the behemoth, "Leave them alone—and I'm not kidding. We'll take this out at EDMONDS STATION." I carefully made sure to enunciate the location of our next stop.

"Oh, yeah...you're a dead man!" He crushed the beer can in his hand to make his point.

Then came the dreaded announcement of, yes, EDMONDS STATION. The car slowed as we approached the platform. I thought I might be able to lure him out and then duck back in at the last moment, but it was a huge risk. The car stopped and I told him to go first. He backed out and egged me on with his fists up, ready to go.

Then, there they were! Four security officers ran up behind him. Those uniforms never looked so good! They nabbed him and dragged him to the ground before I had a chance to blink. Then, the warning tone that the doors were about to close sounded. As I slowly backed into the car, I bumped into the man who'd been behind me. I turned around to see the brother who had my back. I saw a man who stood about 5' 7" and had a slight build. He was white as a ghost, visibly nervous, and had a look of profound relief on his face. Here was a man I did not know, who'd been as scared as I was, and probably wasn't a fighter. Yet still, he was compelled to do the right thing, even when it could have meant physical harm for him. We both looked at each other with a sense of relief and disbelief as to what had just taken place. I took his hand with both of mine and thanked him profusely.

The doors closed behind me and the car erupted as people cheered and clapped. Everyone came up and shook my hand with sincere gratitude. No handshake was more thankful than that of the Indian couple. Their gratitude seemed immeasurable.

I never did get the name of my brother who stepped up that day as he got off at the next stop. I never did see him again. To this day, I have yet to hear words with more meaning and purpose to me as a man than, *"I've got your back."*

It's sad, but some men go a lifetime and never hear those words. Oh, they might hear them bandied about in movies, sports scenarios, or maybe in a bar with the boys. But most men never hear the phrase said by someone who means it. I'll never forget how those words made me feel, and how connected I felt at that moment. Every man needs to have that feeling, no matter where he is in life.

You don't have to be in harm's way to earn those words. When you're in the shits, or when life seems to have you by the short hairs, those four words can make a world of difference. You'll never feel the same as you do when a brother reaches out and says, *"I've got your back."* Nothing can feel more right and true in the moment. This feeling is what it means to be a Remarkable Man.

Brother, I'm with you and I know where you are. If this is the first time you've heard it, or one of many, I want you to know you are not alone. *I've got your back!*

CHAPTER TWO

THE JOURNEY BEGINS

*Man improves himself as he follows his path; if he stands still, waiting
to improve before he makes a decision, he'll never move.*
— Paulo Coelho

If you were to attend one of my seminars or talks, you'd find a man
who is confident, energized, and seems to be having a heck of a lot of
fun. As a professional speaker, being 6' 4" gives me an advantage. I
like to say I was ergonomically designed to be a professional speaker.
I come with my own built-in stage!

However, as tall as I am, and as big as my personality can be, I felt
small for a great deal of my life. I wasn't born with any talents to
capitalize on. I didn't come from a wealthy family, or have a mentor
who changed my life and showed me the way. So, fellas, for me to be
authentic with you, I have to give you my truth, a glimpse into my
journey to becoming a Remarkable Man.

I was born September 4, 1965. I was number two behind my sister,
Karen. My parents were part of the working class. My dad was a
heavy equipment operator, and my mom stayed home with us kids.
Back then, it wasn't unusual if a woman didn't know how to drive.
In fact, to this day, my mom has never driven a car (unless you count
the time she *tried* to drive and put our '65 Beetle in the brambles).
Enough said. Our lives were simple and we didn't lack for much.
We moved around as my dad climbed the ladder and put in time in

small towns, usually because no one else wanted the postings. It was okay, though. Mom was a city girl and cursed the day we moved, but we enjoyed the experience. Over time, my dad's increases in position and pay allowed us more travel and luxuries, and my mom was eventually okay with our nomadic lifestyle.

As a young boy, I was unusually shy, and I missed my parents tremendously when they left for conferences or weekend trips. I was anxious about their wellbeing. I was baffled because I worried so much. Nothing traumatic had happened to warrant such a level of anxiety. However, by the time I was in high school, I manifested reasons to worry. I was a victim of bullying and lacked the self-esteem to confront my tormentors. I was a tall, gangly boy, good-looking, based on what the girls said—but I didn't see it. Not for quite a while.

Most people equate height with excelling in sports, especially basketball. Well, there's another side to the coin. You see, I grew so fast from age thirteen to sixteen (close to eleven inches) that my physical body could not keep up. I became clumsy and awkward. I had chronic lower back pain. My coordination was crappy; I had arms and legs "all over the place," yet no vertical jump to brag about. It embarrassed me to lumber down the basketball court and attempt a lay-up. We didn't have a made-for-Hollywood teaching or mentoring system, either. There wasn't a coach to see my potential, take me under his wing, encourage me, or change my life forever. That didn't happen, so the kids continued to tease me. I soon hated my height and created a mental image of wanting to be smaller than my then 6' 2" frame would permit. I had that "tall kid" droop in my shoulders.

Things changed dramatically for me in the summer of 1982. That's when I met the new, popular guy in town, "Chase." I know the name "Chase" conjures up images of a country club pretty boy wearing a sweater tied at the neck, polo shirt with the collar flipped up, pressed khakis, and designer shades while driving away in his Beamer. No, not this Chase. This Chase usually appeared with beer in hand and a wad of chewing tobacco in his lower lip. He wore a t-shirt, jeans, and a black "Cat Diesel Power" baseball cap. He had a reputation as a fighter, and he worked at area ranches during the summer break. Ironically, my sister, whom I detested more than life itself back then, was dating him. But wait; it gets better!

One night in early July, my friends and I were at the drive-in. Chase sauntered up to the car to chat with my buddy Dene, who was sitting in the driver's seat. Seems everyone knew Chase but me. As Chase talked with Dene from outside the car, he peered in, spit tobacco from the side of his mouth, squinted to look at me through the green glow of the dashboard lights, and barked, "Hey, what's your name, dummy?"

I was stunned and didn't appreciate his offensive greeting. "Who are *you* calling *dummy*?" I blurted. "And what's it to you, anyway?" Chase just looked at me and smiled wryly. He spit out of the side of his mouth, and then, with his left hand supporting his beer on the car roof, he put his right hand into the car past Dene's face, formed a gun with his fingers, pointed at me, squinted, and pulled the trigger. "*Pow,*" he hissed, then blew the imaginary smoke away from his fingertips. He looked at Dene with a knowing grin and quietly said, "I gotta roll. Have fun."

With that, he walked to a car two rows back. Dene looked down, let out a deep sigh, and shook his head.

"What? What the hell was that about?" I blasted.

Dene looked at me with a foreboding look. "Shit, man. You gotta watch your back. Now Chase wants to fight you!"

If you've been bullied, then you know those words just have a way of ripping you to shreds. Drive-in? Movie? What movie? I was so frightened I couldn't have fun with the boys. I seemed to keep living through familiar scenarios I projected into my world. *How did I find myself here? Why do good people like me attract bad people like Chase?*

That summer was hard to get through. Within days, the entire population of 800 knew about Chase's desire to fight me. Okay...the entire teenage population knew. "He's gonna kick your ass" was the phrase being tossed around. It was somewhat surreal because the boys I knew divided into two groups: Chase's Boys and Dwayne's Friends.

The surreal part was Chase and I didn't even see each other most of the summer, so the two groups kept the lines of communication open. Most of the chatter was, "Hey, Dwayne, when ya gonna fight Chase?" Or "Chase can't wait to kick your ass!" Or the classic, "Why don't you fight Chase? Are ya *chicken*?" That was all I heard for weeks.

Finally, while out riding my dirt bike, I ran into "The Boys," and again the question was posed. "Hey, Dwayne...when ya gonna fight Chase?"

There's a time in every boy's life when his mouth ignores his brain and acts on its own. I felt separated from reality as I sat on my dirt bike and watched them mouth the familiar taunts through the chin guards of their helmets. Then, in frustration, I burst out with, "It's on for 6:30 tonight at the park. Be there!" With that, I gunned the throttle, pulled out the clutch, did my best "180," and roared off toward home.

My thoughts flew. *What have I done? This can't be happening. I just accepted Chase's challenge! I'd even added, "...be there!" as if it were **my** challenge! What was I thinking? Clearly, that wasn't my voice! Where'd that come from?* It felt as if my heart were going to pound right out of my chest! My mind was a torrent of so much self-disparaging junk that I rode the four or so clicks home on autopilot.

I quietly cleaned up after I put my bike and gear away. Dinner was ready, and I was worried about being at the table. My folks were oblivious, arguing because my sister wasn't home for dinner, and they didn't know where she was. I wasn't hungry. Then, the basement door closed. It was Karen. She entered the kitchen in a whirlwind of teen rebellion. Before my parents had time to lash into her about being late, she looked at me with a Cheshire Cat grin and sneered, "Chase is going to kick your ass, you loser!" With that, she glared at our bewildered parents, defiantly stated, "I've already eaten," and stormed out to a waiting car.

Okay, then…the cat's out of the bag and the whole town knows. Great! My burnout of a sister wants to see me get my ass kicked. That was no surprise. We truly hated each other. We lived in different worlds and plotted, on a regular basis, to kill each other. This was a happy day for her because someone else was going to do her dirty work. I knew she'd been part of the group that pushed Chase to fight me. A guy wants to impress his girl, you know.

My sister and Chase were the classic ranch town couple—young, rebellious, and cruising around in a pickup truck. You know the one; it's a 1978 Heavy Chevy with gun rack, bench seat, tinted back window, "Back Off" mud flaps, and AC/DC cranked to full volume. Yeah, the stereotype existed in my town too.

Now, my parents were concerned. Their "baby boy" was about to get his ass kicked. My dad looked at me with a somewhat apologetic, but proud, look on his face. "Just keep your guard up and wait for your opportunities," he said.

Oh great—Dad's going to give me fighting tips now. At the last minute! At that time, my dad and I were not as close as a father and son could be. Until I was about twelve years old, my dad was my giving, loving hero. I fell asleep on his lap most nights as we watched TV together. But things changed as I entered my teens. He was still a good provider, but he was more focused on work, dinner, the newspaper, TV, and yard work. The "bonding" was infrequent and I was pretty much left to discover life on my own.

"Yeah, Dad," I said nervously while playing with my potatoes. "I'll do my best."

My mom was beside herself. She glared at my father. "He's going to get hurt," she exclaimed. "How can you let him go off and fight like this?"

I had a different type of relationship with my mom. She was a nurturer; and she lived for her kids. However, once my sister went to "The Dark Side," she focused all her mothering on me. It was so extreme that she was smothering me. I was over-coddled and realized I'd become a wimp because of it. I wanted to break free from the bonds of both my parents because I hated their unique style of parenting.

That day, both parents were visibly concerned. They knew their boy wasn't a fighter and was about to get another one of life's lessons.

Later, and somewhat in a daze, I found myself walking to the park. It was ten minutes of heart-pounding, soul-stealing terror. I'd been bullied, picked on, sucker punched, teased, tormented, and shamed a lot in my young life, but this was a real fight. I was going to be in a fight with a ranch hand who was three years older than me, a loose cannon, an "I'm gonna kick your ass" kinda guy.

And then, the park entrance loomed dead ahead. Its log archway gave way to a beautiful pond, a wading pool with a fountain, a gazebo and all-weather picnic enclosure, a playground with all the usual equipment, and a new "adventure" playground. A creek, spanned by arched bridges, meandered gently through the property. As I walked along the path toward the first bridge, I realized a crowd of kids had gathered. It's amazing how young we are when we first experience bloodlust. Kids as young as seven were in the park to see this fight. We had an audience. Did they think it was going to be an epic battle, with two foes squaring off to settle a score? Or had they come just to see Dwayne get his clock cleaned?

As I approached, I didn't see Chase and "The Boys." Instead, my friends gathered around me. They tried, in vain, to comfort me and pump me up. I briefly thought Chase might not show. Could it be possible? Just then, I noticed the kids were looking past me. I knew he had arrived. I felt him. I turned around as Chase and his crew crossed the bridge. My heart now out-pounded the semi-trucks gearing down as they came into town.

He's bigger than I remember. I hadn't seen Chase since the weekend at the drive-in almost six weeks before. *Maybe he'll be reasonable and we can talk this out.* That all went out the window as I felt the intensity of his energy. He was coming at me quickly. *Oh, crap. This is it! We're going to fight.*

I put my hands up to prepare for battle. As a side note, you're also supposed to plant your feet lightly and keep your balance low. Did I know that? No! Chase came right at me and tricked me. He faked a right punch, and I went for it! But instead, he swung his left leg around and swept my feet out from under me. I landed hard and fast—on my ass. Then, in one glorious moment, everything was revealed. Chase was coming to attack, and everything slowed down. There it was: my moment in the sun! As he came at me, his groin area was exposed! I pulled my right leg back, and with all I had, I launched it forward and up to give his family jewels a rude farewell. I felt my leg uncoil with speed and purpose. It was going to be sweet.

I was already basking in the glory of the moment when my body decided to inform my brain about an unfortunate occurrence. My foot had missed its target! *I missed? At least I got part of him, right?* No, it was a clear miss, a whiff, a huge strike-out! *I missed. No! How could I miss? They...they were right there!*

At times like that, you just know the day isn't going to go quite as well as you'd hoped. *Let the carnage begin.* Everything went bad for Dwayne. I was in a very vulnerable position, on my back, on the ground. Chase was easily able to strike from above. I "turtled" to protect myself. Yeah, I wasn't much of a champ! I felt his fists hitting my face and head. I knew they were hard hits, and my head snapped back and recoiled from every blow. Surprisingly, I didn't feel much pain. It was happening too fast. I was out of the fight before it began. But Chase's killer instinct wouldn't let up. Something was different. He was brutal in his quest for victory. He kicked my face, head, and stomach. Punch-drunk, I felt his boots kicking tufts of hair from my scalp. He then pulled me to my feet and said, "We aren't done yet, asshole!"

I could hear him, but I couldn't see him because my left eye was swollen shut and blood blurred my right. The crowd's chants of "Fight! Fight! Fight!" seemed to give way to a noticeable uneasiness as he continued his assault. Soon, I heard the crowd begging him to stop. He continued, using my face as fodder for his pent-up torment, holding me up by my collar with one hand and driving his point home with the other. Finally, I heard a man from the neighboring trailer park coming over, yelling to stop the fight as he approached. Chase suddenly dropped me and fled into the crowd. The impacts stopped.

Is it over?

My body slumped over to my right as I struggled to get to my knees. My head felt the size of a basketball. My face was hot from the swelling and cuts. Half aware, I heard the man scolding the kids. "What's wrong with you people?" he demanded. "Get the hell home!"

My friends got me to my knees. I could see out of one eye that the crowd had left. Slurring, I asked my friend Doug, "How ish it? How do I wook?"

Doug replied, shaking his head and sighing, "It's bad, man…bad."

The man wanted to get me to his place so he could call an ambulance. But my friends pleaded with him and said I'd be okay. Reluctantly, he left us there and returned home. Doug grabbed a garden hose that was nearby and handed it to me. I ran the water over my head, soaking my hair. The water was cool and soothing. The puddle forming beneath me was red with blood. I was startled at the amount of blood flowing and pooling in the puddle.

The vision in my right eye was clearing. I looked toward the picnic hut and saw my sister and her friend sitting on a glassless window-sill. She actually looked sad and sorry for her brother. Just seeing her there triggered a hatred I'd never felt. Knowing she could have stopped Chase's attack and didn't caused a darkness to surface from within. All I could muster through my swollen lips and bleeding mouth was a low and guttural, "I'll never forget this." I looked at her with contempt and loathing. And while I didn't say it, I'm sure my eyes did. Yeah, I blamed her for this assault.

My friends took me to Doug's place, where they got me cleaned up and brought out the ice packs. Some serendipity revealed itself. The guys thought my teeth had been smashed in, but it was just blood from my cut lip. Most of the cuts were superficial. I didn't need stitches, and my nose wasn't broken. In fact, after we washed my face and applied bandages, we realized I just had a swollen lip; one eye was swollen shut, and there were lots of small cuts on my scalp. I had sore ribs and bruises on my torso. And oh, what a headache. I went home late that night since I didn't want my mom to see her son all beat up.

My strategy didn't work. My parents were worried and had stayed up waiting for me. My mom was in tears when she saw me, and my dad was very concerned. Still, it looked like he was proud of me. My mom's tears kinda got to me, and I remember some emotion welling up in me when she gave me a hug. *Nope! I'm not going to cry. Suck it up!*

"Mom, I'm fine, really. I'm just tired and want to go to bed."

That night, I had at least four ice packs going and Neosporin covered every cut and bruise, which was most of my body and face. My head felt like it was covered with lumps and bumps, and my pillow felt as comfortable as a cement slab. A few cuts, I reckoned, could have been stitched because they were quite deep. After an hour or so of trying to get comfortable, I drifted into a sound sleep.

I woke up to the sound of a lawn mower across the street. It was another beautiful day. My dad was already out watering the flowers before the sun's heat got to them. Slowly, I made my way to the washroom and began my Sunday morning routine. When I went to wash my face, I remembered I'd been thrashed just shy of my life only a few hours earlier. I was shocked when I looked in the mirror. I leaned into my reflection to understand what I was seeing. It wasn't what I expected to see. It was a miracle! My eye was swollen and black, but it was open just fine. The bridge of my nose was a bit swollen, but it wasn't the mammoth snout I'd seen the night before. The cut on the inside of my lip was tender, but manageable. The cuts on my cheeks were hardly noticeable and the deep scratches on my head were scabbed over and hidden by my hair. Yes, it looked like I'd been in a fight—a week ago!

I went to the kitchen to pour some cereal. When my dad walked through the back door, he was floored. "Wow! I can barely tell you were in a fight. Lorraine! Come here," he yelled for my mom. She came into the kitchen, drying her hands. Seeing her, he smiled. "Check out our boy."

She turned toward me, let out a big sigh of relief, and then quickly switched gears to scold me. "Don't you ever put me through that again!"

When I finally made my way downtown that day, it didn't take long to realize the whole town knew I'd been in the fight of my life with Chase. People couldn't believe the lack of evidence of the intense beat-down I'd suffered. The rumors had ballooned. Apparently, I'd been sent to the hospital. I had broken bones, no teeth, and a broken nose! So when people saw me, they couldn't put the rumors together with the reality. At least I got a little support from the Universe on the back end.

CHAPTER THREE

MY "MCFLY MOMENT"

Only to the extent that we expose ourselves over and over again to anni-hilation, can that which is indestructible arise within us. In this lies the dignity of daring. We must have the courage to face life, to encounter all that is most perilous in the world.
— Karlfried Graf Durkeim, philosopher

Six weeks had passed since the fight. Everything seemed to return to normal. The intense adversarial energy between our cliques dissipated. My eleventh grade year was just underway. I was in a new school since our town did not have a school facility for eleventh and twelfth graders. We rode the bus thirty minutes to the next town. With the new school came a new energy, a new beginning, and a chance to reinvent myself. I made new friends, and a group of pretty girls actually noticed me. Not that I would act on it. No, I was far too insecure to chat with the girls.

I found out about a tradition, an event that was the buzz around school: the "Pre-Grad" party. It was a big outdoor blowout that celebrated the last school year for kids in twelfth grade. Of course, all the kids went, and it was a huge party. It took place in the hills, just outside our town, far from the public—and the police. My friends and I got there early to help set up. The area was called Donut Valley. It was a perfect place for a party, a dry lake bed up in the hills, surrounded by a forest of Ponderosa pines. The bonfire went in the center, and there was parking for hundreds of vehicles. I was excited about partying with my friends.

It's interesting how quickly things can change. We got there that night at about eight o'clock and enjoyed setting things up with a few of the older, and cool, guys in town. I felt like I was in a new clique. I belonged. Then "Chief," a friend from school, showed up. He was of Aboriginal descent, hence the nickname. He was a man-child in every sense of the word. He had a poor school record and had repeated grades a couple of times. He was stocky, tough as nails, and had a mean streak you did not want to cross. He was an "enforcer" on the junior hockey team. Oh, I almost forgot—he had been a member of Chase's entourage a few weeks back.

Chief was laughing and handing beer to the guys, but when he got to me, his energy changed abruptly. He coldly walked past my waiting hand and muttered something that sounded like, "Watch your back."

Great! Just great! My excitement suddenly shifted to dread and confusion. My mind started rolling. *Does Chief mean he's going to hurt me, or is he warning me of someone else's plan? Nice. I thought this crap was over.*

Cars, trucks, and old beaters came up the two winding, dusty roads into Donut Valley. *Looks like there's going to be a crowd.* Two pick-up truck beds held the concert speakers. Once the generator was fired up, AC/DC, The Cars, Cheap Trick, and Pink Floyd shook the valley.

As darkness overtook twilight, the bonfire grew to inferno proportions, pushing the revelers out and away from the heat. You could always spot the loners or those who'd had too much to drink by the way they gazed hypnotically into the heart of the fire. About six-hundred kids were enjoying various stages of inebriation and partying. However, I still had an uneasy sense that *not* all was right with the world. I got a vibe from certain cliques that they knew something I didn't.

As Doug and I talked with a couple of friends from my new school, I saw, out of the corner of my eye, that the crowd was parting. The fire was at my back. Its heat was so intense you couldn't stay in one position for too long. At least I could trust the fire to be there. As the crowd grew closer, I could tell Chief was making his way toward me. He was a raging bull, drunk beyond recognition, and mad as hell. I didn't see the friend I knew; he didn't exist. He'd been possessed by alcohol and his anger was in control. He grabbed the collar of my favorite baseball shirt. The sudden lurch up hurt my neck.

"Time to die, Klassen," Chief slurred, spraying my face. Negotiating out of this situation was futile. Everyone knew Chief wanted to fight me and the chants were on.

"Fight, fight, fight!"

"C'mon, Chief; kick his ass!"

"Punch him! Kill him!"

My reputation as a fighter had spread since I'd been pummeled by Chase not so long ago. I was an easy mark. I guess I was someone you could fight to earn points with your clique or boost your ego. I was about to get a beating and there was nothing I could do about it. Or so I thought.

There are times when seemingly impossible circumstances call for equally impossible actions. The moment was upon me. Something happened in a brief, but life-altering, moment. As Chief held my collar and squeezed even tighter, I felt the collar of the shirt begin to tear. At any moment, Chief's angry fist would find my face.

I felt like George McFly in the movie *Back to the Future*. McFly is helpless against tough-guy Biff, who knocks McFly aside to have his way with George's girlfriend. Then something comes over McFly. His hand finds a way to make a fist; he musters the strength to stand and confront Biff, and then...*Bam!* McFly clocks him with a right hook that knocks Biff off his feet, out cold!

I became George McFly. Time as I knew it slipped away. The blood-thirsty, chanting crowd disappeared from my mind. I held Chief away with my left hand and my half-empty beer bottle with my right. A voice I'd never heard took over. Without taking my eyes off Chief, in a calm controlled voice, I said to Doug, "Here, hold my beer."

I sensed Doug's astonishment, and I knew he was looking at me with wide-eyed surprise as he cautiously took my beer. With my right hand free, I formed a fist. It was now or never. I was 6'3" at the time, which gave me some advantage. My fist had to cover a long distance, but it moved fast and true. At impact, I realized it was the first time I'd ever landed a punch on someone's face. The blow was so powerful that I saw the big guy fall back. I was stunned. In that moment, I felt a massive shift in energy. I was overtaken, possessed by energy that had been buried for too long. It was rage, anger, deep hurt. All the years of torment and struggle for acceptance exploded to the surface. As Chief landed in a cloud of dust, I jumped on him before he had a chance to react. I was calculated, cold, and mean. I aimed punches at his eyes, mouth, and nose. Every blow released my pent-up pain. I didn't want to win a fight; I wanted to end the cycle. I don't remember how many times I hit him as he lay there groaning, bleeding, and unable to withstand my fury. At some point, my friends pulled me away from him. I was in a huffing, panting, crazed, testosterone-filled daze. Their physical touch snapped me out of my spell.

What have I done?

My friends' faces said so much. There was disbelief in their eyes, like they didn't know who I was.

I looked down to see Chief rolling and gurgling in pain in the dust and darkness. The crowd quickly formed between him and my line of sight, and he was swallowed up in the shadows. With shock and trepidation, the crowd shifted its attention to me. When people spoke, they uttered words I'd never heard about myself.

"Did you see that? He kicked Chief's ass!"

"Wow. Klassen beat Chief!"

Then slowly, cautiously, people approached me. They treated me like I was a wild animal they just wanted to touch for the first time.

"Hey, man, that was cool. You sure know how to fight. Get this man a beer," shouted one of the "cool" kids. Girls I'd deemed out of my league looked and grinned coyly my way.

It was hard to take into account what had happened. I turned to my friends and said, in a broken voice, "I need to hit the trees. I'll be back in a second." I worked my way over the logs and past a few fir trees, far enough into the forest that the crowd wouldn't see what was about to happen. I didn't need to relieve myself. My bladder wasn't full. Something came from deep inside me. Like a beaver dam bursting in flood season, a torrent of emotion rushed up from within and could not be contained. I leaned forward against the trunk of a large Ponderosa, and touching it with my forearm, I buried my head in my dusty shirtsleeve. And then I bawled. I released the emotions of what had just happened. The adrenaline was overwhelming and had me shaking. I wept in a happy release of the pain and suffering I had endured. I knew I had just broken free from an old self. I knew my life was changed in that moment, and I cried.

After a few moments, I collected myself and made my way back to the party, where I was a real part of the scene, not relegated to the shadows. Standing tall, I felt alive. Suddenly, the crowd again parted before me. It was Chief! He was moving quickly toward me. *Does he want a rematch, a chance to redeem himself? I thought this was over.*

As he emerged from the shadows, he was almost unrecognizable. His eyes were almost swollen shut, his nose was visibly broken, and his lips were cut and huge. Blood was crusted over with dust. As he approached, I noticed his energy was different. I tightened up and readied myself for the worst, but he stretched out his big arms and hugged me! He then slobbered loudly into my ear, "You kicked my ass! Awesome, man! We need to have a beer!"

Okay, it's a guy thing, but that night changed my world. To give Chief credit, I would not have stood a chance if he had been sober.

I'm not proud of my "McFly Moment" since I've never understood the need to fight and deliberately hurt someone. However, I'm proud to say I haven't been in a fight since that night. However, the Universe had to take me there and give me a scenario that pushed me to show up in life instead of being a victim. I didn't understand the message at the time, since my awareness hadn't yet developed, but the synchronicity was profound. It served me well once I was wise enough to comprehend its serendipity.

At school the following Monday, I wasn't the Dwayne I'd been before. The kids' attitudes had changed, and they actually wanted to associate with me. The bullies and tormentors suddenly looked small, scared, and insignificant. That fight with Chief was not a Remarkable Man moment. However, it was a dramatic shift that earned me a measure of respect. I didn't feel like a different person. I was not in my ego. I was still self-conscious about who I was, but that fight allowed me a personal freedom I'd never felt before.

CHAPTER FOUR

LIFE SHOWS UP

People often say that this or that person has not yet found himself. But the self is not something one finds, it is something one creates.
— Thomas Szasz

I wish I could tell you that my life after my "McFly Moment" was one of confidence, strength, and direction. I wish I could tell you it was the beginning of my Remarkable Man transformation. But I can't. Back then, I wished people believed that, and for a time, I embellished my life to avoid looking at my world.

After high school, I went to college to become an architect, but I realized I wouldn't benefit from my artistic flare until after I completed the program's engineering component. I just didn't have the moxie or drive to go through seven years of school to make it happen. My lack of confidence in my math skills prevented me from going beyond a civil engineering/drafting diploma. I hated the experience and realized I was heading into a career path that was wrong for me.

From that point, I was drawn to sales, an interesting choice because it went against my personality. I was an introvert and felt extreme anxiety before sales calls. In my anxiety, my rectal muscles tightened so severely that the sharp pain made me catch my breath. If you've ever had a Charlie horse in your calves, then multiply the pain by ten! And remember, the pain isn't in your calves. There was no way I could talk until I was able to relax enough to let the pain subside.

It was a challenge since these attacks usually happened when I was driving.

Strangely enough, I was good at my job once I got in the door. I had a natural talent for getting people to feel comfortable. My sincerity and product knowledge built trust easily. I never had to use the "slick salesman" approach some of my colleagues used.

I worked in music management, carpet cleaning, car sales, bartering, publishing, painting, and more. I can't say I made it to the million-dollar roundtable or won all the sales awards. At best, I had marginal success in most of my endeavors. I could have been a top producer, but I wasn't. You see, I was handcuffed to mediocrity, with an occasional moment of brilliance and performance. I didn't believe in myself. I didn't see what my managers and colleagues saw. I went to every sales training program and read every book I could get my hands on to snap out of it. Yet nothing seemed to help.

One day, a friend came to me with two tickets to an Anthony Robbins seminar. He said, "Hey, you're into this self-help crap, right? You want to go?"

I was excited. "Anthony Robbins? Are you kidding me? I'm there!" As it happened, another friend had loaned me his boxed set of Tony Robbins' "Personal Power" program just a week earlier. I was consuming it with great enthusiasm, so this opportunity to check out my new personal growth hero elated me!

We were seated about two-thirds of the way back in the conference center, but it felt like we were in the front row. Tony's energy and charisma were electric, and the whole audience was caught up in a wave of potential and possibility. I marveled at how Tony commanded the stage, how the audience was hungry for his gems of information. He was a master, and I was in awe. The fact that he wasn't much older than me also intrigued me.

Then, the strangest thing happened. Out of the blue, my friend elbowed me gently, leaned over, and, without losing sight of the stage, whispered, "That could be you, man. I can see you doing that!" My friend, who knew all about my personality and challenges, was telling me that Dwayne Klassen could be a world-class motivational speaker!

I responded with a half-audible and perplexed, "Really?"

My friend didn't even hear me. As the program continued, I was only half-aware of what Tony Robbins said or encouraged us to do. I was pondering my friend's comment. I superimposed myself up on the stage instead of Tony. I visualized my powerful delivery as I shared my heartfelt stories, my pain. I saw the audience laughing and having fun. I saw the lights go on in their eyes as another powerful point hit home. I saw it all—my future, my calling, my destiny.

I set out to learn everything I could about becoming a motivational speaker. Someone suggested that joining Toastmasters International' would be a good first step, a way to learn some fundamentals of the art of public speaking. Toastmasters? I'd heard about it, but I didn't know what it was. I thought it was one of those secret society groups like the Freemasons, or the Skull and Bones. I thumbed through the phone book (we didn't have the Internet back in the "Dark Ages") and found a Toastmasters chapter that met within walking distance from me.

Turns out, the chapter had one of the largest memberships in the district. When I arrived, several enthusiastic members greeted me warmly and introduced me to other equally enthusiastic members. Thirty-six people attended that evening, and I felt good as I observed the proceedings. Then came the segment called "Table Topics," in which the leader selects three people at random to go up to the front and give an impromptu talk about a subject, with no time to prepare. You have to speak for two minutes, and then group members critique you on structure, including the opening, body, and closing of your speech. To make matters worse, they count your speech fillers, like "um," "ah," and "you know." I enjoyed watching the first two speakers have a go at it, and surprisingly, they were very good. Then, I felt an energy that suggested I would be next. As the leader scanned the room for the final speaker, the two men on either side of me pointed at *me* to be the next choice.

"Dwayne," he said, smiling, "would you please come to the front?"

As I got to my feet, group members applauded and continued to do so as I made my way to the stage. When I turned to face the group, I felt my heart pounding and my hands sweating profusely. My clammy handshake must have earned an "ick" or "yuck" in the leader's brain.

The topic was something along the lines of, "Does a class system exist in today's world?" I only had a few seconds to ponder the question, and then the clock started. I don't know where it came from, but my mouth just started going. It felt right to be up there, speaking in front of the Toastmasters group. I was surprised at how naturally my words flowed. Before I knew it, an amber light warned me that my two minutes were almost up. I drew my talk to a conclusion and followed the closing protocol of the previous two speakers. The lively applause was like a drug or tonic I'd never experienced before. It's sad to think that some people go through life and never receive applause. It's quite a rush, no matter how large or small the crowd. I received applause for the first time that day, and I LIKED IT!

As I returned to my seat, the men seated next to me gave their support and said I was a natural. It felt strange, in a great way, to receive so much encouragement in one night. As the meeting ended, they announced the best speech, best table topics, and best evaluator for the night. Each winner received a beautifully embossed ribbon. Wouldn't you know it? I received the "Best Table Topics" award! When I returned to my seat, the man to my left leaned over and whispered, exasperated, yet jokingly, "I've been here for three months and I haven't received that thing yet!"

So there it was, my first speaking experience, the first rung on my ladder to become the next Tony Robbins. I knew I had a gift, and my destiny was beginning to unfold. I could see my future. By regularly participating in Toastmasters and honing my skills, I was confident I'd be there in a couple of years.

Of course, that meant I'd need to take action. Do you think I returned to Toastmasters the following week? Nope! Did I go back the week after that? Nope! Did I ever go back? No! I did not return to that Toastmasters club. It would be three years before I went to another meeting. Such a tragedy. I knew I was a good speaker who'd be able to soar, but I didn't take action.

I realized I was good at many things, but my strongest self-sabotage mechanism—*my ego*—said, "Dwayne, you know you can be successful, famous, wealthy, and happy beyond your wildest dreams, but where would that leave me, your ever-faithful ego? Do you think you're fooling anyone? We're a team. Don't you remember? Dwayne, you've gotta return to the *real* world. Remember, you're shy, insecure, and weak. *You need me.* Look at your friends; they're just like you. If you follow through with this self-growth stuff, you'll have to leave them behind. Remember, making new friends is scary. It's better to hang onto what you have. At least you know I'm here for ya, pal."

My ego was cunning, sharp, and convincing. I let go of my dream, and instead, I pushed through a life of mediocrity. Through this mediocrity, I even manifested the demise of my car sales career. Yep, I was good at that! You see, I'd received a few awards and corporate jackets along the way. So, following my ego's direction, I slacked off and became a middle-of-the-pack guy. I took shortcuts, gave less care and attention, and backed off on my formerly impeccable customer service. It didn't take long for my ego to get me to a place where I was no longer happy as a car salesman. Just months before, I'd been on fire and jazzed up about going to work every day to "see tail lights," even on my days off! Now, I made up excuses, put blame on other salesmen, and got caught up in cliques and backstabbing with some of my co-workers. I soon left the industry. I said it was a sleazy business and I was too good to be a part of it. In reality, I enjoyed the car business. The training and people were top-notch. I didn't experience the stigma of Herb Tarlek, the sales manager on the sitcom *WKRP in Cincinnati*. I just stopped showing up as a true professional. My negative self-talk and attitude manifested the environment I found myself in.

It got worse from there, much worse. After my car sales career ended, I took too much time off and lived off my savings. I realized I was in financial trouble. I finally got a job, but it would be three weeks before I received my first paycheck. Unfortunately, I didn't even have enough money to buy necessities to survive until then. I was too embarrassed to ask my family and friends for help. My options were limited, so I decided to go to the local welfare office. It was humiliating to be in line waiting to register for my allowance, especially since I'd been living large just a short time before. I realized I'd reached an all-time low. In my mind, I remained defiant. *I am not one of these people! This is crazy! How have I allowed myself to get here?*

Then, just when I thought it couldn't get any worse, I had to cross another painful threshold. My last government welfare check was supposed to arrive in my mail. I had too many bills and no food. I was waiting with anticipation for the letter carrier to arrive so I could cash the check and breathe again. I saw the letter carrier through the window. I leapt to my feet and went around to the front of my house. The carrier had just left the yard as I quickly opened the mailbox and reached in for that familiar brown envelope. My mind sorted through the mail as fast as my fingers could go. *Pizza flyer, Realtor flyer, phone bill, grocery flyer. Come on, where's the check? Maybe I missed it.* My heart was pounding. *Try again, Dwayne. Pizza flyer,*

Realtor flyer, phone bill, grocery flyer. No, no, no! It's not here!

My head was pounding; my breath was short and shallow. Panic-stricken, I could barely return to the house and hold back my emotions. I slumped onto the couch and allowed the mail to spill to the floor. I stared down at the mail scattered on the rug at my feet. My hands made their way to my heavy head. I could feel it coming. Oh, could I ever! I lost it. I mean, I just lost it. I sobbed long and hard! I was angry with myself for not having control of my life. *How did I get here? Why didn't I take* action? Then I became angry with God, spitting mad with Him, for not helping me or answering my prayers. Alone and betrayed, I wailed away with indignation and contempt. As the pain intensified, my tears flowed with ever-deepening sobs. After ten minutes of letting this torrent of hurt flow forth, I became philosophical and began to ask questions aloud to myself. *Why was my pain threshold so low that I had to experience such depths of despair and anguish? Only a few months earlier, I'd been at the top of my game and thought I'd be a world-class speaker. Why must I experience pain in order to act and move forward? What am I so afraid of?*

As I poured out these questions in a mess of tears, snot, and spit, I turned my head to the side and noticed the Tony Robbins "Power Within" series on the shelf next to my stereo. It seemed brighter and more obvious than it had before. I sniffled loudly, caught myself in mid-sob, and began to understand the gift in the moment. A laugh crept out from under the crying. Another sniffle and another smile emerged as a wave of hope and love came into my soul and body. *I got it! I got the gift! Ha! "Power Within," that's the sign. It's all inside me!* A wave of euphoria came over me. I felt a new sense of self and was overwhelmed with the feeling that everything would work out just fine. I looked down at the mess of mail and noticed the corner of a brown envelope stuck in the grocery flyer. I reached down and pulled it out. *Could it be? Yes! It's the envelope from Social Services!* I tore it open in a blur. It wasn't the check I desperately needed. Instead, Social Services was notifying me that my check was waiting for pick-up at their office. There'd been a clerical error and they needed me to pick up the check and sign a document to indicate I no longer needed assistance.

I laughed uncontrollably, not at the relief of knowing my check's whereabouts, but at the silliness of my little—okay, *big*—outburst. I hadn't cried like that since that night in the forest after I fought Chief, so I knew I'd been holding in a lot of negative energy. I thanked God for this gift; and I felt a bit stupid for railing so hard at things beyond my control. I was also glad that Tony Robbins' program was on my shelf. I think I got more out of seeing the cover of the box at that crucial moment than I did from the contents it held. Then, when I realized the positive neuro-associations I'd learned through the program had triggered my new awareness, I knew Tony Robbins' program had influenced me. I vowed I'd never again allow myself to go to that level of pain, despair, and lack of control.

Before that day, I'd set my "energy thermostat" low, and I manifested a vibration to match the frequency of my thoughts and beliefs. I was caught in a world of mental laziness, and as a result, I couldn't even provide for myself. My self-esteem was gone. I'd given away all my power. Most of the people in my life at the time were in the same boat: jobless slackers, complainers, and burnouts. I'd known some good people who enjoyed life, but over time, they'd blocked me from their world. They didn't do it with words, but energetically. As you've probably heard, like attracts like, and the positive people I'd known didn't want my negative energy to manifest in their lives. If you've been to this level, then you know what I mean. I have many gifts and talents, but in that period, I forgot who I am and what God has given me. Despite signs from the Universe that I'd find support if I just trusted myself more, I'd allowed ego and my small self to take control.

CHAPTER FIVE

CAN I BE REMARKABLE NOW?

Every great dream begins with a dreamer. Always remember,
you have within you the strength, patience,
and passion to reach for the stars to change the world!
— Harriet Tubman

Let's fast-forward to the period I thought was the greatest time of my life. I didn't feel this way because my life was filled with joy, ease, and abundance, but rather because it was during this period when I experienced the greatest lessons for growth and for writing *The Remarkable Man*.

It's interesting to see how our lessons show up. Usually, we only get the gift in hindsight. It's hard to recognize a gift when it's wrapped in the guise of traumas, setbacks, or major life challenges. Unless we're fully aware, it's difficult to appreciate what we experience as it's happening. Oh, I talked a good talk about being a man who was aware, awake, and on the right path. In fact, most people I knew thought I had a good way of handling my lessons with grace and poise. Many told me they were amazed at how unfazed or calm I was in situations that would cause them to "lose it" or be depressed or angry. Yes, I expressed my thoughts and feelings, but I was muted in a big way. Despite outside appearances, inside I was hurt, sad, lonely, and afraid. I was not being authentic about myself. I wanted the world to see a man who had it all together. Yet in truth, even after twenty years of self-help, transformational education, and insight, I was just like everyone else.

I hit a new low in 2004. I was in bed in my mom and stepdad's spare bedroom. I'd just left a relationship and was in transition. We'd broken up and she was seeing new men before I'd even moved out or found a place to live. Yes, she was dating before I was even out of the house. That's how little she respected me. I moved in with my mom and stepdad to get away from that. Yes, I know I allowed it. Yes, that was a low place.

Anyway, I was reading *The Science of Getting Rich* by Wallace R. Wattles, and I was eager to change my circumstances. I'd always dreamed of being a multimillionaire and knew that someday, somehow, I would get there. As I read the book, I realized I needed to have a big plan in order to get from where I was to where I wanted to be. But what could I possibly do to succeed? I went to sleep every night with these concerns running around in my head. Then one night, the Universe gave me an answer, and it had been right under my nose for a long time.

Many years earlier, I had developed a concept for a unique outdoor advertising medium. It had promise, potential, and the makings of a global venture. But alas, the lack of maturity or business acumen needed to pull it off wasn't there, so it died a quiet death. However, that night, the Universe told me to resurrect it, start fresh, and see what happened.

The next day, I shared my plan with my folks, and they were thrilled with my desire to pursue it. Within days, right there on the kitchen floor, I built a full-size prototype of my outdoor advertising concept, the Curb Cap™, the idea I'd had almost fifteen years earlier. When it was finished, I was quite pleased with how cardboard, glue, tape, Plexiglas, and some paint made it all come to life.

I went to the managers of parking lots that would be potential clients and asked whether they'd be interested in advertising if Curb Cap were available. Eighteen of the twenty said, "YES." They loved it, and thought it was innovative and clever. Buoyed by the results, I began to create a business plan. A week after completing it, my friend Jim Lotwin (a Remarkable Man) was so impressed with the potential that he invested $10,000 to get it going. Just like that! Yes, within three weeks of having the idea, I had $10,000, and more was coming! This funding started the beginning of a new life and an amazing adventure.

It was December 2005. Now it was real. I was proud, excited, and visualized becoming a media mogul. The business had legs, we'd raised more than $1.2 million in start-up capital, and were expanding into Las Vegas. I saw nothing but blue skies ahead because I had some value-added concepts to add to the mix to grow the company even more.

I'll get back to the business story in a little while. You see, while I was growing the business, a side story was building. During the company's first two years, I took weekend trips to the coast each month to visit the most important person in my world, my son. We weren't a perfect family, but since I'd manifested it, I made the best of it.

Wait. Let's go back to the year 2000, when my son's mom and I were dating. We'd been intimate for a short while, but then decided it was best to continue as friends. Some time had passed until one night she called me. I hadn't heard from her in a few weeks, so it was nice to catch up. During the call, her voice became heavy with emotion as she said she had important news. "Dwayne, I'm pregnant."

We hadn't dated each other exclusively, and she'd been away for a while, so—as a friend—I was about to congratulate her and ask about the father. But my happy feeling turned on me when she said, "You're the last person I was intimate with. Dwayne, this child is yours."

Now, I love kids, and I wanted to have children in a big way. But this? Not like this. I was thirty-five years old and about to have a "love child"! It was crazy! The phone in my hand began to shake, and a surge of fear and confusion swept over me. She felt my energy shift. Through tears, she said she was three months along, and she was going to move to the West Coast to be closer to her family. She'd decided to follow through with the pregnancy, obviously, but said it was up to me to decide whether I wanted to be involved in our child's life. I was so stunned and surprised that I couldn't respond right away. She understood, and we decided I needed to take a couple of days before I gave her my answer.

I must have been white as a ghost when I hung up the phone. My uncertainty was based on the fear I'd manifested in my world, and anxiety about what people might say. That phone call changed me irrevocably. I actually vomited from the emotions that wracked my soul. My racing thoughts would not subside. *A child? I'm not ready! It's not supposed to be like this. I need to have a plan, a family unit, a dog, and a house with a white picket fence. What will my family and friends think?* Sick with worry, shame, and guilt, I went to bed that night wondering how I'd manifested this situation.

The next morning, I felt rested despite the life-changing news of the night before. I was filled with a sense of peace, and I wanted to explore its source. Then I remembered a Buddhist philosophy: we choose our parents before we are born in order to learn certain lessons from them and from the situations that will come from being raised in that environment. With this insight, I couldn't help but smile. A feeling of grace swept over me as I realized, "This child has chosen *me* to be its father." I felt gratitude and joy. "I'm going to be a dad!" My eyes welled up and I thanked God for the gift I'd received. I called my son's mom and excitedly told her, "I'm on board. Let's do this!

My son was born that year on September 15. When I held him for the first time, I didn't want to put him down. My financial circumstances weren't good at the time, so I wasn't able to see him as frequently as I wanted. Still, we did the best we could, and as he got older, my situation improved dramatically. Since my business was starting to roll, I could visit him whenever I wanted to or fly him and his mother out to visit me. We had a special father and son bond, and I was richer for it.

Just after his seventh birthday, I was visiting and we took him to soccer practice. It was the first time I'd seen him with his team. Now, when kids first learn to play soccer, they run around in a pack and flail at the ball with little semblance of organization or strategy. It's quite cute to watch. However, as I watched the kids play that day, I observed something that seemed a little bit odd. My son, the little guy near the middle, was the runt of the litter. I don't mean to come across as cruel, but he and another little boy were four to six inches shorter than the other kids in their age group. They weren't just shorter; they were also smaller in build. My son's best friend was about eight inches taller and outweighed him by fifteen pounds or more! I was puzzled, and turned to talk to his mom. "Look how small he is compared to his friend," I said. "He's just a little guy."

His 5' 3" mom looked at me with a matter-of-fact glare and said, "Of *course* his friend is taller! His mother is like 5' 10'!"

Her reasoning surprised me. I looked back at my son and said in retort, "Well, his *dad* is like 6' 4"!"

She got that deer-in-the-headlights look and quickly turned her attention to the game. I enjoyed watching my son play, but my brain was accessing something from a far-off place. It felt like my synapses were misfiring and sparking, like the damp fuse of a firecracker. Then, the low clouds finally gave way to rain. As parents clicked open their umbrellas, worry took hold of me and wouldn't let go. I felt like a boat being pressed into its moorings during a storm. Finally, my mind allowed the thoughts to come into my consciousness and the fuse sparked to a flame. I looked at my son, then at his mother, then back at my son. The rain was coming down hard. My hat was soaked and didn't keep the water off my face. I put my fingers through the wire mesh of the fence surrounding the field and clutched it tightly. The sounds of children laughing and parents cheering diminished to one solitary little being. I could feel his heart racing, his lungs gasping, and his eagerness to play well for his teammates. *There's my little man...my little guy.* The lump in my throat grew as the shocking revelation washed over me. *He's my son....but I'm not his father.*

The sharp trill of the coach's whistle snapped me out of my trance. Practice was over. I composed myself in time to greet my muddy, exuberant, pint-sized David Beckham wannabe.

"Did you see me, Dad? Huh?" he asked. "Did you see me almost get that goal? I was good today, wasn't I?"

I tousled his wet hair playfully. "Yes, Son, you were awesome!" My approval made him giddy.

I didn't say anything to his mom about my thought. At the time, it was just a feeling, not something I could substantiate by discussing it. I had just a short time left with my "Little Man," and I was determined to keep my suspicions from ruining it.

About two weeks later, I was at home, sick with a cold. I just wanted to rest. I stretched out on my couch, got cozy, and watched daytime TV. Actually, what I did was press the remote every five minutes since my attention span was as thin as a playing card. I went through about three channels while my main show was on a commercial break. At the third click, my brain went, "Hey, hold on...back up a second." So I went back a channel to confirm what I'd caught a nanosecond before. It was *The Maury Povich Show*, and wouldn't you know it, they were revealing the results of paternity tests. The show was almost over, and just before the credits rolled, they posted a toll-free number for those who were unsure about their paternal responsibility. Yes, DNA testing.

Before I had time to think, I found myself dialing the number. I was on autopilot. The operator on the other end of the line had a thick Southern accent, and images of the character Flo from the '80s sitcom *Alice* came to mind. She was helpful and compassionate. She said the only lab in my area that provided at-home DNA kits was at the coast, and she gave me the number. I called there and was treated with the same courtesy and support. I was surprised at the amount of counseling the lab provided for fathers or potential fathers. Through their compassion and understanding, I felt it was all right to feel what I was feeling.

I had arranged to visit my son in two weeks, around the third week of November. It was perfect timing because his mother had planned a weekend in Vancouver for herself. That meant "we boys" would have the weekend to ourselves. My usual routine was to fly to Vancouver, get a rental car, and then take the ferry to Vancouver Island. The DNA lab was about thirty minutes from the airport, so it was just a quick pit stop. The counselors I met were helpful and showed me how to collect, package, label, and handle the samples in order to get solid results. It was quite a procedure and protocol, I might add. A shocking statement also was presented to me. The counselor said, "The fact that you are here means that there is a 90 percent chance you are not the father."

My son and I had a great weekend. We hung out at the beach and explored nooks and crannies along the shoreline. We were wild-eyed pirates, superheroes, intrepid explorers, and Star Fleet commanders on a distant planet, and all within just a couple of miles of beach. It was a lot of excitement and adventure for him, and with the sea air, he was always out like a light, fast asleep in the car on the way home.

On my last night with him, I played the saddest game of my life. I helped him with his bedtime routine: bath, jammies, and brushing his teeth. The last part is where the "game" came into play. The DNA lab said it was the best way to get a sample from a child his age, without raising suspicions. We played this game when we brushed our teeth. As he brushed, I put my sample swab in my mouth. This evoked a common reaction. "Whatchya doing, Dad?"

Although I felt horrible about it, I answered, "I'm just checking for plaque to make sure I brushed my teeth correctly."

Then, of course, came his inquisitive response. "Can I try that too, Dad?" I produced a swab especially for him, and *voila*—we'd collected DNA samples, and he was none the wiser. Unfortunately, no amount of counseling prepared me for how I felt as I played "the game". That night, I felt shame and profound sorrow as I tucked my little man into bed, tousled his soft hair, kissed his forehead, and left the door open just a crack, just the way he liked it. "The game" was over, and the next day I'd stop at the lab on my way to the airport. After that, I'd have to wait a month for the test results.

Christmas was approaching and I looked forward to seeing my boy at our favorite time of year. We loved Christmas, as it was a Lego, Hot Wheels, and Thomas the Train extravaganza. As he got older, I had more fun sharing my inner child with him. Every Sunday, we talked on the phone or used video on the computer. He was especially excited this year because of the Batman movie and accompanying toys. I was going to Australia for New Year's, so it would be perfect to spend time with my boy and head "Down Under" from there.

Then, on the day before I was to leave for my visit, I checked the mail and found a large legal-sized envelope waiting for me. It was from the lab. The DNA test results had arrived. My thoughts raced. *This is it. Holy crap, it's here. Open it! What are you waiting for?* I realized I was immobilized; all I could do was stare at the envelope. Then another voice in me spoke in a calm, centered voice. *No. I'm not going to open this…not yet! He deserves his dad on Christmas…all of me. And I deserve my son. We'll have a blast and enjoy our time together.* And we did! It was our best Christmas together, my favorite Christmas with him.

Alas, it was my last Christmas with him.

When I returned from Australia, the envelope was there waiting for me. I could no longer ignore the inevitable. I opened the envelope and nervously pulled out the report. The lab had told me there was no "gray" area. Either you're the father or you're not the father. I took a deep breath and looked. There, printed at the top of the report, were my results: 99.99989 *Not Compatible*.

So, there it was. Those results cut to my very core. My little man was not mine! Anguish and heartache encased me. I held the test results in my hands and sat on the couch. Then, a rhythmic splatter of tears began to hit the paper. All I could think about was my boy. A video of his life played before my eyes. Every happy memory triggered another wave of sadness and tears. I'd never loved someone as deeply as I loved my little man, and oh, did it hurt! My heart was breaking. Then another feeling began to take hold, a feeling that stopped my pain in its tracks. Rage and anger toward his mother took over. *That little bitch! How could she have done this to me? She used me. She knew it all along and she used me! All the years of child support, even though I'd often struggled to come up with it. Our friendship…all of it…a lie!*

I was on my soapbox, angry as hell at her, the world, and myself for having been so naïve and trusting. *What will my folks think? This will crush them!* They were born to be grandparents and lived to see their grandson. He was the twinkle in their eyes.

I was surprised when, upon hearing the news, people said they'd been suspicious all along. Everyone had the same reaction. Of course, they were shocked and disappointed by the news, but told me that deep down they'd felt something wasn't right from the beginning. *Great! So I'm the only one who didn't know?* Well, that wasn't true either; my higher self had given me those thoughts now and again, but I just didn't think it would be true in my case. After all, how could I have thought of anything other than being his dad? Besides, it wasn't as if she were after me for anything. Okay, yes, there was the child support and a good role model. *Oh, how could I have been so blind?*

So, what was next? I wasn't his paternal father, but that didn't mean he needed to suffer. The friendship I'd had with his mother was over, but I was the only father my little man had ever known, and he needed his dad. I decided to continue to be his dad, despite this devastating revelation. It felt right, and it was.

When I confronted his mother with my sad and infuriating discovery a couple of weeks later (it had to be in person, no phone call or letter could suffice), she was shocked to learn I'd found out and sorry for what had happened. She'd known he wasn't my baby, but she had felt I was the best choice for giving the child a good father. I expressed, in no uncertain terms, that our friendship was over. However, my boy should not lose a father because of her deception. She understood, and she was glad I'd still be there for my boy.

This arrangement worked for about three months, and then she slowly started to make it difficult for me to see him. As a man without a father's legal rights, I was left to her whims. She moved to Vancouver that fall, and sadly, I haven't seen my little man in more than three years.

You'd think that finding out your child isn't yours would be more than anyone could take. However, I still wasn't finished with the lessons I needed to learn. Remember my advertising company? Let's get back to that.

While business was going well, I sensed a shift in the company's energy. We had to let our CFO go over a side deal he'd been developing with a potential manufacturer. They were going to overcharge us and split the overage with the CFO. Needless to say, we didn't choose that manufacturer. The fiasco cost the company dearly and set product development back six months. Even more, I lost a friend, since I'd trusted him more than anyone in the organization. Then, the drama got bigger.

It's interesting to think about the people we manifest in our lives. Through my own naivety and trust, I manifested a team most would see as good people. Yet nothing could be further from the truth. I wish I'd read *Snakes in Suits* by Paul Babiak and Robert D. Hare before I'd started down this path. I had surrounded myself with a team that was anything but focused on moving the company forward. I soon realized two of the officers were alcoholics; one was "functional," the other was not. Once they found each other's vice, they became a coalition willing to undermine my authority and enable their addiction, all at our shareholders' expense. The amount of money they'd spent on booze junkets and personal items was shocking. As their lack of productivity and absenteeism increased and their excuses became more elaborate, I began to investigate "The Boys."

As part of my investigation, I learned our VP of Corporate Affairs had been disbarred after stealing more than $40,000 from Legal Aid. He'd been a criminal lawyer, and used all the tricks in the book to skirt my authority, not to mention his fiduciary duty to the company. Our VP of Sales was another smooth operator. I'd been led to believe he'd been involved, at a high level, with some of the most recognized corporations in North America. I learned he had a criminal record for domestic violence and theft. Since he'd been recommended by a friend, we hadn't done any due diligence on him. As it turned out, he certainly wasn't the man he said he was. There's a lesson here. Always do background checks and don't rely on a friend's recommendation, no matter how close you are.

Now, it wasn't all bad. I did have a few bright people in the company. My office manager and a couple of sales associates were professional and loyal, not only to the company, but to my vision. They saw the challenges I was facing and recognized the blatant contempt their bosses had for the shareholders and me. They did their best to let me know about the schemes and behind-the-scenes plotting of my demise. Through the grapevine, I learned that "The Boys" wanted me gone so our shareholders would never know about their unrestrained spending and lack of accountability.

Finally, I took my evidence, and along with three employees who'd seen "The Boys" in action, I met confidentially with two board members I thought I could trust. They reacted to our presentation with surprise, concern, and irritation. By the end of the meeting, both had committed to helping me get "The Boys" out of the company. On the way home, we were excited about the direction the company would take once the plan was in place. Unfortunately, our enthusiasm diminished quickly. Not more than a day after that confidential discussion with the board members, word of the meeting came from one of "The Boys." He told me they knew everything, and based on what he said, I had to agree. The board was playing us—and we'd fed them all the details. Sadly, two other board members, one being a company Vice President, were in camp with "The Boys." The board members were convinced that if they didn't go along with "The Boys," they would be just as responsible for the shady business and lack of accountability. Too scared to accept the truth and join me in telling the shareholders what was happening, they decided it would be easiest to remove the thorn in their sides. And so, in September 2006, to shut me up, the board acted on an illegal vote to remove me from the company I'd founded.

I was devastated and enraged. The people I'd trusted had betrayed me. When I sent letters to the shareholders, they were shocked to learn I'd been removed from my own company. At the same time, "The "Boys" started a campaign to undermine the trust and credibility I'd developed with the shareholders. They portrayed me as an ego-driven maniac, out to fire everyone so I could have the company all to myself. I had "Founderitis," they said. They were very convincing, and ironically, they used company resources to keep the shareholders from meeting so they could hear the truth and vote accordingly.

An ugly and costly eighteen-month legal battle ensued. The shareholders didn't know the truth until finally, I found an ally in the then-new COO. Incidentally, he'd also been wrongfully fired, essentially for finding out too much. He'd wanted to know why I was no longer with the company and why the company was spending so much money to keep me out. He never got a straight answer, and upon uncovering the financial mismanagement, he sounded the alarm—only to be fired a few days later. He and a major shareholder sought me out to get the truth. With their help, we finally had our day in court and won the right to hold a shareholder meeting.

In that meeting, we won by a landslide with more than 90 percent of the vote. We gained the sharcholders' approval to clean out the board and officers and turn the company around. I was excited to be back at the helm of my company and have it go in the direction I knew it could. However, my enthusiasm was short-lived when we realized it was a hollow victory. After auditing the company, the truth became painfully clear. We were far in debt and the skeletons left in the closet were too much to overcome. We could only keep the doors open for six months. What was once a promising and exciting global venture was gone.

The nineteen months leading up to the victory in court were difficult, and they cost me more than my company. I fell into a state of depression shortly after my dismissal. The truth about my son, combined with the loss of my company, was too much for me bear.

I was engaged at the time, and my fiancée was gorgeous, tall, and vivacious. She had a smile that could melt hearts. She was self-sufficient and had worked hard to get where she was. I believed she was my true soul mate. However, as wonderful as she was, she wasn't equipped to handle a man who needed help finding his way back.

The ugliness of the legal battle included threats to my safety. I was living with her and her two beautiful girls, and the threats came too close to home. I didn't want my struggles to cause them any worry or fear. As a "family," we weren't on a solid foundation at the time, and I could feel it. The masculine energy I'd once had in spades had become little more than a flicker. I felt emasculated, half the man I'd once been.

Almost a year into our engagement, we decided it would be best for me to move out until things improved. Unfortunately, I knew that once I moved, we'd never be the same. And we never were. We were friends and saw each other now and again. She was a rising star with her employer. She traveled extensively and had visions of moving east to the company's main office. A strong, independent woman aches for a man who'll be at her station in life, or better. I knew I couldn't be that, and letting go was the best thing I could do for her.

Guys, I'm not sharing my past because I want your sympathies. I'm sharing my past because I want you to understand that I've been down that road—with all its bumps, turns, and blind corners. I've made my way through many challenges. I didn't understand why bad things happened to me as I experienced them, even though the answer was there in front of me all along. I faced all those seemingly tragic events so I might have the insight, experience, and firsthand knowledge to pass along to you.

The Universe has always wanted me to be Remarkable and let my "big self" come through. I just wasn't ready. I wouldn't have had any credibility with you if I'd just read a bunch of books and gone to a bunch of seminars. After that, I might proclaim myself an expert, but I'd only be able to regurgitate what I'd learned. People would see right through that. I needed to show up and break through on many levels in order to be an example of what it takes to overcome adversity, trauma, and pain.

I fully understand and appreciate the fact that many of you have endured more pain, hurt, and challenges than I have. I created The

Remarkable Man because I wanted to challenge you—the guy who knows there's a better life waiting for him. It's my calling to encourage, guide, and cheer you on as you make your way to your own vision of being a Remarkable Man.

PART TWO

REMARKABLE TRUTHS

CHAPTER SIX

KNOW YOURSELF

If you insist on clinging on to who you are right now, you will miss the extraordinary opportunity to meet the next greatest version of yourself.
— Debbie Allan

The path to becoming a Remarkable Man is unfolding before you. However, I must warn you. This journey is not for the faint of heart. This is man-sized work that will take man-sized effort on your part.

This chapter is about getting real with who and what you are. It's about examining the truth before you figure out how to change any behavior patterns that don't serve you. I'm not going to pull any punches with you. You—okay, your ego self—may not like what you read. Being Remarkable means taking action, not just physically, but mentally, emotionally, and spiritually. I had to dig deep and snap out of a self that took almost forty-three years to create. Your own digging is about to begin.

Changing your life is actually a very simple process. Yes, it's very simple, but that doesn't mean it's going to take place without some struggle. I'm not going to pawn off a quick fix here. It took you years to get to this place in life, so it's going to take some time to leave it behind. Let's kick it off with a bang. I mean, why waste time waiting for your ego to get angry? Why don't we do it right now? Are you ready?

The person you are right now, in this very moment, is NOT the person you know you want to be. It's true! Oh, you can lie to your-self and say you've got it going on, everything's great, and you're a self-actualized man. However, if you were going to do that, then you wouldn't have picked up this book. Also, you wouldn't have had the negative thoughts, feelings, and emotions you've experienced throughout your life. How's your ego doing so far?

I know many of you have success, love, and happiness in your life, and I applaud you for getting there. I'd love to know about the jour-ney you took to achieve your bliss. However, I'm going to guess you're still looking for a missing piece of the puzzle, however small it might be. Now, if your ego's still in check, we're still in good shape.

Let's begin with a positive, yet provocative, set of questions:

- Are you living a life full of purpose?

- Are you excited about your future?

- Are you a man in his full power?

- Are you on fire to start another amazing day when you wake up in the morning?

- Is your relationship with your wife, partner, or girlfriend thriv-ing, exciting, and sensual? (If you have all three of these, then we need to talk.)

- If you're single, do you enjoy being single? If not, why? What is keeping you from feeling that way?

I'll let you ponder those questions, and your answers, for a few mo-ments. I want to get one thing straight before we go any further. This book is not going to give you any foo-foo, Pollyannaish, or mystic advice that makes you put your tongue in your cheek because it just won't work in your "special" case of real life. Some of what you read will be familiar because it just is. These pages contain ancient wisdom.

There's nothing earth-shattering here. The difference is in how your "other selves" interpret and integrate what you've learned at this time in your life. Now is when you need it all to come together. When I refer to your "other selves," I mean exactly that. Many "selves" make up your personality: your happy self, sad self, greedy self, dark self, hurt self, victim self, courageous self, leader self, suffering self, brilliant self, foolish self, and so on. Did I miss one of yours? How many selves exist in *you*?

What you are about to read is everything I did to become Remarkable in life. I'll be honest with you. Writing this book has been a challenge because I'm writing about myself while I'm still a work in progress. This is especially true since I don't have a stellar record to share. Remember, no superstar status or huge claim to fame here. I'm just an inspired guy with one hell of a vision: to influence the lives of millions of Remarkable Men! If that's not being called to do something big, then I don't know what is.

When I told my friends I was going to write this book, some of them were skeptical and gave me that look of, "Oh, great. Dwayne's got another one of his crazy ideas." It wasn't the rousing support I'd expected, but I understood their doubts. After all, I didn't have a reputation for showing up in my life. However, those who knew of my gifts, talents, and passion said I was doing what I was meant to do. Their support was, and has always been, endless.

Okay, now that I've given my long, drawn-out disclaimer, let's get back to those questions. Did you forget about them? Let's review:

- Are you living a life full of purpose?

- Are you excited about your future?

- Are you a man in his full power?

- Are you on fire to start another amazing day when you wake up in the morning?

- Is your relationship with your wife, partner, or girlfriend thriving, exciting, and sensual?

- If you're single, do you enjoy being single? If not, why? What is keeping you from feeling that way?

Know yourself. It's the first step on your Remarkable journey. Who are you? A man with purpose and passion is unstoppable. You know those guys; there's just something about them. Perhaps you've been there before and have gone from knowing what you're *supposed* to be doing to actually *doing* it.

Have you finally experienced such frustration, pain, and lack in your life that you're willing to begin, and stay with, the process of becoming a Remarkable Man? Remember, it's simple, but it won't be easy. It will require effort and desire that must be greater than anything you've felt before. I request your commitment. Decide today that you truly want to be a Remarkable Man.

I'm sure that as you read these words, you are nodding your head and thinking, "Sure, I'll commit." But due to the magnitude of this journey, I need you to do more than nod your head. I need you to take an action step. This step will create in you a symbolic and tangible commitment to becoming a Remarkable Man. In order to stay on track and follow through, you need to sign a pledge. You do, and it's for your own good. Trust me. It works!

You can fill out the pledge in this book, but I recommend that you download the "Remarkable Man Pledge" from our web site: www.remarkablemanproject.com. Then click the "RMP Pledge" link near the top of the page. That way, you can print and display it in your bedroom, bathroom, den, office, desk, or anywhere you might need a daily reminder of the journey you're taking. It's also great to share with your wife, girlfriend, partner, and children to let them know you're dedicated to being a champion and hero in their lives. So... stop reading. Take time now to print it out and sign it. Come back when you're able to see and read your Remarkable Man Pledge.

I know many of you would prefer to read until the end of the chapter before you do any exercises or assignments. However, if there's any possibility you might be able to interrupt that pattern, now would be a good time. If you can't print or fill out the pledge right now, I encourage you to stop reading until you can do so. It's important to get the ball rolling in the right direction, and it starts with your commitment to yourself. Don't worry; the words will still be here. I'm serious! Stop reading, mark this page, and do it now! Make that pledge to yourself. You can do this. You're worth it.

Welcome back.

Most of us can talk about changing our habitual patterns, but when it actually comes to getting started...well, that's a tough one. I understand. Let's start with a simple exercise. Oh, relax! It will take only a few seconds and you'll feel better for it. Ready? Place this book on a surface that still allows you to read it. If you can't put it down, try holding it in one hand. Now, I want you to raise your right hand high (if you can't, then use your left hand). Hand up? Okay, now reach behind your head and over to your opposite shoulder. Reaching? Good! Now give yourself a nice pat on the back. YOU DESERVE IT! You've made the decision to be Remarkable, and that's worthy of some self-praise! Umm, if you're still patting your back, you can stop now. Don't overdo it just yet. You're just beginning, so don't get too cocky. There's much work to be done.

The truth is that most of you are living a half-life, unsure what to do to make anything better. You fizzled out when you were twenty-five years old, and you'll spend the rest of your life in a zombie-like daze. You're one of the sheep, part of the huddled masses, an automaton just hoping to get through the week. It's not all your fault; society has given you a false sense of what life and reality are all about. Even if you consider yourself aware, you must admit that the world we've created, this earth school, isn't always a cakewalk.

Sometimes it feels like it's a curse to be awake and aware. Understanding who and what we are often hits harder when we forget our power. We become frustrated, sad, angry, disappointed, lonely, afraid, and so on. We realize we're knee-deep in the paradox of the life we've created. Each of these emotions is a sign and a reminder that we are not our God-selves. We're not being present or connected. To make matters worse, there's the obvious fact that as men, we aren't wired to recognize and use our emotions to manage the lives we've manifested.

At your core, there's a sense of whom you long to be. If you're required to work for someone, statistics say that 70 percent of you are unhappy in your careers. Sure, you might be one of the few who loves your job. You know yourself better than anyone does. However, if you're unhappy in your job, then why do you put up with it? The answer isn't complicated, really. You're there because of your fear! We'll take a deeper look at fear in a later chapter, but for now, just realize you're afraid of what might happen if you exchange the known (and familiar) for the unknown, even if you're miserable. You're afraid that if you go after your dreams and desires, then the bills won't get paid because the check you rely on every two weeks won't be there.

There are two reasons for not following through:

1. Fear of success, and

2. Fear of failure.

I had the double whammy. I was afraid of both, but I went after my dreams anyway! As one Remarkable Man to another, I challenge you to take *one step* today toward your passion. What web search could you do? Who could you call? What task could take you one step closer to making your dream come true?

Don't make up a bullshit excuse or lie to yourself about why you can't do this. Instead, get going! In order to begin this journey, you need to understand your purpose, your calling. To achieve what you desire, you must believe in yourself so much that no one or no circumstance can knock you off course.

Starting today, make a few simple inquiries or take one step toward your purpose. I'm not telling you to quit your day job or shirk your responsibilities. However, if you *can* quit and move on to your passion without it negatively affecting your life, then go for it. In fact, I wouldn't even call it quitting because a Remarkable Man doesn't quit; he sets himself free.

Let's assume one of the reasons you're reading this book is because you know you have a purpose, a calling, a gift to share with the world, but you aren't sure what to do or how to do it.

Let's say you've always wanted to be a writer. Is that enough to get you actually to sit down and begin the novel within you? I doubt it! No, you need more than that. You need to have a vision of your life and what writing will look like in that life. Writing in itself is great, and if you're talented enough to enjoy writing any chance you get, so much the better! If not, get the fire going within yourself and show up as a writer by getting more clarity as to what a writing life looks like. What would you enjoy writing about? What kind of writing do you like? There are so many options to choose from: books, magazine articles, children's books, freelance, romance, science fiction, self-help, spirituality, history, and more.

In order for your purpose to compel you to write and see it through to the end, you need a sense of vision. What result do you desire? Let's say you want to be a famous published author. Okay, now you have something the Universe can work with. Let's start with the end in mind. Envision every detail of your life as a famous published author. One of my heroes, Wayne Dyer, uses a unique tool in which he creates the cover for his book first. He mocks up the design, and then wraps the cover over an existing book. This way, it looks like his next book is already published. Then he works to see it through. It's a great tool to "pre-pave" your intentions. I did the same thing with this book and even posted a photo of my book on Facebook.

Visualize yourself listed as number one on the bestseller list. See yourself on a morning newscast. See yourself on a worldwide book tour, speaking to thousands of fans. Whatever your compelling desire, you need to see it as already happening. Search within to discover why you want that which you desire. If your desire is to be a writer, then the biggest question of all is, "Why do I want to write?" What message do you need to share? What makes you believe that you, and only you, have that particular message? You may not be skilled as a writer, but if something inside you says you must write, then listen to it! Begin at once to learn all you can to share your message with the world.

My biggest challenge is that I'm easily distracted. At times, I find ways to sabotage my efforts on an hourly basis. Writing this book was no small feat for me. I work out of a home office. My cat adores me and vies for my affection any time he can. I have great friends, a Facebook account, and I enjoy YouTube. I live in a dynamic city with lots of activities just outside my door. So I have all these distractions, and very little discipline to ignore them at times. But here's the truth. The book wasn't going to write itself. It was always only as complete as the last page I typed. No self-help, mind mastery, meditation, or affirmations were going to type one letter on a page. I had to do it myself! Strange how we think the words will just come without effort. Okay, I'll own it. I admit I thought I could do it without effort.

I had a choice. I could choose to have a book "sort of" started or kinda done. More likely, I could've procrastinated it into the heap of "almost books" I'd attempted in years past. Or I could choose to listen to my higher self, my calling, my purpose by blocking out time to write. During that time, the distractions would need to wait while I focused on the task of moving closer to completing my book. That block of time might be two hours, a half-day, an evening, or a lunch break. I've gone to coffee shops with my laptop to get a change of scenery or to find inspiration. I had to overcome my tendency to become distracted, and that wasn't easy to do. A part of me was in my ego, as I wanted to be one of those entrepreneurs who wrote an epic book while sipping lattés all day. Problem is, many of my friends and acquaintances are self-employed and have meetings in coffee shops too. Sometimes I'd end up in a gabfest, and unless I cut the visit short, I wouldn't get anything done. So I warn you about writing in areas that have a lot of distractions.

Set a goal to write a certain number of pages per session. If the words flow, then keep on writing. Don't stop unless you have to. You may find that in moments of inspiration, you've written several pages beyond your goal. That's when you're truly in your bliss. That's when it seems effortless.

While I used the example of being a writer, you can plug any desire into this scenario. If you dream of being a business owner or have a great invention you want to get to market, the same rules apply. When I started a game company with my sister years ago, or more recently with my advertising business, I had to write a business plan. It was a long, tedious, and frustrating process. However, it was not going to write itself. Sure, you can pay someone to do it for you, but I highly discourage you from doing that as a first step. Your heart and soul must go into your business plan. You need to know everything there is to know about your new venture. Your business plan is your research, your library, and your guide for success. Doing it yourself gives you the satisfaction of a task completed and you know the details intimately. This energy is then transferred to your investors, who will invest based on the ROI, but mainly because of their confidence in you to get the job done.

Once again, it won't get done unless you persevere and start writing, doing the research, and getting excited about the pro formas and projections. Every day, complete one little part.

Do you want to know why it's important to live with purpose? It's simple, really: The world will begin to move *with* you, not *against* you. You'll find yourself at peace with your place in life. And any woman will tell you, nothing's sexier than a man who knows himself. You stand tall, shoulders back, and have a stride that says, "A Remarkable Man is walking here."

Much of a man's energy is in how he holds himself. You hold power and charisma in your chest, shoulders, and back. Contrary to what you may think, your power is not in your pants! In fact, *that* head will get you in more trouble than you can imagine. If you want authentic power and energy that speaks volumes to others, then learn to walk and breathe like a Remarkable Man. Your physiology can make a huge difference.

Here's another exercise, another step. Stand in front of a mirror where you can see your upper body. Relax your shoulders and arms. Now take a deep and confident breath. Inhale. Straighten your back and bring your shoulders back. Your chest should be puffed out or more exaggerated. Continue to breathe deeply and confidently. Watch how your physiology changes. Notice how much more confident you feel as your posture improves. This feeling is your true charisma. There's a reason your mom always told you not to slouch.

A person judges you within seconds of seeing you. Very few men carry themselves properly. In fact, many of us walk around with the weight of the world on our shoulders—and it shows. Just taking a few seconds to be mindful of your breath, shoulders, and overall posture will help you regain your energy and charisma. In any given moment, ask yourself, "How would a Remarkable Man carry himself?" Then do it! Women will notice this too. Boy, will they ever!

My friend, you are greatness personified. And during the time we have together, I am going to prove to you just how amazing, powerful, and Remarkable you are.

CHAPTER SEVEN

THE ILLUSION AROUND YOU

*A mind focused on doubt and fear cannot
focus on the journey to victory.*
— Mike Jones

Let's take a quick snapshot of the world in which you live today to put into context the challenges, obstacles, and issues you're facing. As you know, some energies move you forward and other energies pull you back. In today's world, there is a lot of pressure on men to be, do, and have more. It's a journey fraught with obstacles, both real and imaginary. Explore this imaginary world for a moment because most of your ghosts, challenges, and fears are born in the unseen.

Your personal fears are one thing, but what if something were going on behind the scenes to perpetuate your fears? That's crazy talk, right? I mean, what outside force or system could be so powerful as to induce feelings of fear in your life?

Well, it's everywhere. Look at your finances. Do you have any fears wrapped around money? Of course, most people do. In fact, now more than ever, there is extreme angst about where the economy is going. The world is going through an economic shift unlike anything we have seen. Do you remember a time when the word "trillion" seemed like a fantasy number? It was just too big to comprehend. We associated it with the number of stars in the sky or grains of sand on the earth, but not money. Today, it's a common number, frequently thrown around for bailouts and debt. One trillion is one-thousand billion! It's a number you don't want to know about, yet the U.S. debt is close to $53 trillion. Yes, that's a real number—not the phony $13 trillion or so they want you to believe. Do some of your own digging on that one and you'll see; truth is stranger than fiction.

The current economic situation may be hitting you in many ways, but it stems from one major energy vibration and one you have control over. You guessed it...fear! Fear is driving this meltdown. Fear is the primary weapon big banks use to drive companies or community banks into receivership or bankruptcy. The media is part of a campaign to make sure you feel uneasy and concerned about your nest egg, investments, and economic future. And guess who owns the media? Yes, the banks! Fear is powerful, pervasive, and takes you off your game in a hurry. Fear sells, wins ratings, lowers your guard, makes you more malleable, and takes away your power.

If you are a man with money problems due to the current economic mess, I sympathize. I could write an entire book detailing my own experiences with lack and scarcity.

Money is an illusion. Some of you might be shocked by what you're about to read. Do you remember the trillion dollars we discussed above? Do you think that money is sitting in a bank vault waiting for withdrawal? Hardly! It's not even there! Today's banks don't hold a lot of actual physical cash. Everything happens electronically. It's nothing more than numbers on a computer screen. There is maybe four dollars in real cash for every hundred dollars on deposit. The trillion dollars does not exist. It never did! It was created out of thin air and given value by a system that's almost a hundred years old.

If you really look at the concept of money, you'll see it has no real value, except what society (the banks) places on it. Are you always chasing money, always wanting more of it, and losing sleep because you don't have enough of it? Do you feel powerless when you don't have money? Do you feel like a king when you do? You aren't alone. As a man, you're wired to connect your self-worth with your net worth. But remember, money in and of itself is worthless. The hard truth is we don't want *money*. No, we want the experiences and feelings that come with having money. In other words, we want what we can get in exchange for money. We need to look at money as an energy exchange. Money is just a currency for ideas, feelings, and experiences, get it? **Current + Energy = Currency**. In truth, your net worth is *not* a reflection of your self-worth.

If you assess your self-worth according to how much money you have in the bank, you are foolishly attaching yourself to nothing. It's just a bunch of numbers on a screen. Your so-called wealth is not actually there. It's all just thin air, an illusion on the grandest of scales, and we've all bought into it. I know it might be hard for some of you to grasp the concept of money not being real, but I encourage you to do your homework on the banking system and the Federal Reserve. See for yourself just how silly this whole game is. I could go into detail here to back up what I'm saying, but that isn't the purpose of this book. I merely want to plant a seed to help you to get away from the "slave to money" mentality. A lot of information about money is available via the Internet, books, magazines, and more. As an Internet search, enter "the truth about banks" or "the creature from Jekyll Island." Or have fun with it and just type "economics + lie" in your browser and see what comes up.

I'm not trying to scare you or jump on a conspiracy bandwagon. I'm simply encouraging you to seek the truth for yourself. Once you educate yourself about the truth of our monetary system (it's the same worldwide), you can become detached from the headlines, lies, and economic crap that's being forced upon you by the media. You'll know it's all a game at the highest level, and none of the economic collapse or uncertainty is by chance or happenstance. It's all by design, and all for the controlled movement of capital and power.

Once you understand the mechanism, you'll never watch the news the same way. You'll be able to see past the headlines and know that the bad news, misleading polls, and money prices are all an illusion designed to keep you in fear. But as a Remarkable Man, you are above that and can be more objective because you know the truth. In fact, I encourage you to stop watching TV in general, and the news in particular. If you have to watch the news, ask yourself these questions about every so-called news story:

Who benefits from this story?

- Is it me?

- Is it the person on camera?

- Is it a corporation?

- Is it the government?

If you don't benefit from the story, put up your filters and detach from it. There will always be "real" news—weather disasters, fires, mishaps, and of course, the token feel-good stories near the end of the broadcast. However, in most cases, the following categories will not benefit you:

- Government

- Medical/Health

- War

- The Economy

- Law

- And...wait for it...*Sports*!

I know what you're thinking. "Did he just say sports? How can my Remarkable brother say *sports*?"

Sorry, guys, but it's true! Now, I'm a big sports fan. I love hockey, football, golf, and auto sports. But, I have to be selective about how much time I allocate for sports. Becoming a Remarkable Man meant freeing up time to devote to my passion. Watching sports on TV had to get to the point where I only watched my teams in crucial games or in the playoffs until I finished what I needed to do.

People use sports as one of the biggest "go back to sleep" tools out there. If you're tuned into sports for three hours at a shot, I guarantee you won't be working on your purpose. And the system will thank you for it. Think about it. Whether your team wins or loses, how much do you gain personally? Nothing! No growth, no progress, no new awareness. Sure, if you're a stats guy or in a sports pool, you might gain some knowledge or win or lose a bet. However, when it comes right down to it, the only people who benefit from sports are the people on the other side of the camera.

Yes, we're guys and that's what guys do. We watch our warriors conquer the enemy's warriors. It brings us closer in victory and humbles us in defeat. Shit! You buy that crap? Come on, wake up, man! Enjoy sports for what they are, but don't do it because you're a man and that's just what you're supposed to do. That's old-world thinking. Surely, you want more in life besides looking forward to "Plaaayyyyzzzz of The Week!"

Advertisers know the weakened state of a man's mind while he's watching sports on TV. They bombard him with images that lower his intelligence and sense of identity to something ridiculous or impossible for the average guy.

Women know about this ploy too. They do! She'll come down to the man cave while you're watching your game, knowing how tuned-out you are. Oh, you've experienced this, have you? She'll make a few "I want" or "I need" statements and you won't even hear them. Your brain is functioning at such a low level that you cannot engage her fully. Your attention span is narrower than the edge of a ruler. Any interruption causes your ego to react rather than respond. So you tell her something you hardly thought about, just to appease her and shut her up so you don't miss a play. She either uses your lowered state of intelligence as a way of testing you, getting mad at you again for an unresolved issue, or for getting her way. Oh, women know what they're doing. Advertisers know it too. Wise up! You know exactly what I am talking about.

Sure, watching sports on TV is fun and I'm not saying to give it up. I'm just saying that when you're living for your purpose and have decided to play a bigger game in life, you will make a choice either to move forward or to stay where you are.

Here's something to ponder. Next time you've watched your game on TV, ask yourself, "After three hours of my precious time, who really won? Was it my team? Was it the advertisers? Was it the owners? Or was it me?"

I've digressed. Yes, the media creates great spin, but it has an agenda to promote a certain vibration. It's focused on creating fear, worry, guilt, scandal, control, and shame. We hear all the time that the news media is unbiased and objective. How can it be objective about a medical story when its advertising dollars come from a pharmaceutical giant?

The illusion is based on fear. Understanding fear can be a huge step toward your personal freedom. Fear is small and dark due to an absence of light. Fear is scared of the truth. Most of all, fear is never a match for love and authenticity.

Even though we're in the midst of fear campaigns by the illusion masters, the very systems that exist to perpetuate fear are breaking down. Institutions and corporate giants are crumbling to their foundations. Yes, it may appear that they are strong and seemingly unstoppable, but their time is running out. And they know it.

This shift is one of the reasons I wrote this book. We're waking up to a truth that's both beautiful and sublime. This awakening will only intensify. Because of this shift, it's imperative that every one of us start to see how Remarkable we really are.

You may be wondering about this "shift." I'll explain. For millennia, the world has been governed by a masculine energy. This energy is about dominance, control, fear, and suffering. Most of the pain on this planet today is brought about through masculine energy. Hear me out. I'm not saying the pain was brought on by men. I said it was brought about through masculine energy. Man is just the vehicle to carry out the agenda.

Feminine energy has suffered during this period. I'll go into more detail about this topic in a later chapter, but it is important that you become aware of this, as feminine energy is returning to the planet in a big way. The faster you integrate this awareness into your consciousness, the faster you will become a Remarkable Man.

Through this book, I'm working to raise your awareness of two types of masculine energy. One will move you forward in unmatched strength, courage, love, and purpose, while the other will pull you down into ego, pain, suffering, and ignorance.

Manifesting your dreams, goals, and desires will get easier as this shift gathers momentum. Your success with the women in your life will improve dramatically as you begin to understand this energy shift. The illusions that have kept you from your purpose will begin to break down. It will become easier to tap into your genius and the true nature of who you are. The illusion will collapse, the curtain will fall, and you'll know the truth. It's flawless in design and the timing is perfect. The world's vibration is changing dramatically from masculine to feminine. It's been shifting for years and we're going to witness an epoch in history in our lifetime.

The great thing is, you already know this stuff. You've sensed it for a while now. Now that you're on the road to becoming Remarkable, I challenge you to minimize your TV viewing. If you must watch news of the world, watch it with new eyes, ears, and awareness. You'll be more at peace with what you see, and you'll understand what works or doesn't work for you. If you're truly fulfilling the purpose in your life, you won't have time to waste watching the news. You'll be far too busy enjoying your passions and what matters most in your life.

CHAPTER EIGHT

TIME

Much may be done in those little shreds and patches of time which every day produces, and which most men throw away.
— Charles Caleb Colton

We all have the same amount of time every day. A billionaire has the same number of hours on the clock as you do. World leaders, the winners of last year's Super Bowl, and celebrities all get the same number of sunrises and sunsets in a year as you do. These people, and others, have amassed great success because they manage their time effectively.

Logically, this should be the point where I tell you I'm a master at time management. Well, that's not going to happen! However, I've become better at managing my time, and I'll share those strategies with you shortly. Until a short while ago, the life I'd created for myself was the product of not being a good steward of my time. I squandered hours, even days, on indecision, inaction, and distractions; it's no wonder I wasn't where I wanted to be. I've always recognized my time management challenges and constantly looked for ways to improve. I had the latest time management books, downloads, and schedules from the gurus and leaders, but nothing seemed to work. I'd start a time management program with enthusiasm and could stay focused for maybe a week. And I would see results. But inevitably, I slipped back into my old time-consuming/time-wasting habits that stalled or impeded my progress. In fact, writing this book took me along a familiar path. I started with great gusto and excitement, and before I knew it, I'd written almost seventy pages. Then, like clockwork, my old self surfaced to help put off my writing.

Can you relate to this situation? How often has it happened to you? How many times have you had a project that started well, but somewhere along the way, you ran out of time? Many of the people I talked with regarding this book also viewed TIME as their nemesis. We have become slaves to time, rather than being masters of time.

With the shift in energy on this planet, your mastery of time will become more important. As the vibrational shift in manifestation gets stronger, time will either work for you or against you. Have you noticed that the time between thought and manifestation is getting shorter? So be mindful of your thoughts, since the law of attraction will work for you or against you, based on your perspective. The law always gives lavishly, in accordance with your thoughts. Become aware that the period from thought to manifestation no longer gives you the buffer zone you once had. So if you're constantly stuck in a negative thinking mode, be prepared for more pain and suffering, as it will happen quickly. I prefer to focus on the positive side. The period between positive thought and positive outcome is getting shorter too.

I'm the kind of guy who bought into the idea that I need a certain amount of structure in my life. As it turns out, I wasn't alone. Most men think this way. I need to plan my day, and that makes sense. Planning my schedule—and following through—has dramatically improved my results and effectiveness. Lately, though, my accomplishments aren't just a result of better time management. Rather, it's because I have a deeper understanding of time itself.

At one time, I was known as a poor time manager, and I had evidence to support this reputation. I needed to understand why time didn't work on my behalf. Why was I always hurrying, or getting things done at the last minute? It's because I was fulfilling the beliefs of a guy who *thought* he didn't have much control over his time. You see, language is a real and powerful force, and you must be aware of it. If you say certain words frequently enough, your subconscious mind will believe they must be true and project the energy you need to experience it.

If I were going to be a Remarkable Man, this thinking had to stop. I needed to become a master of my time. So I dissected an entire day. Not any specific day with an agenda in mind, but a normal, twenty-four-hour, day. Have you ever stayed awake for twenty-four hours? It's an incredibly long time. My admiration and sympathies go to those of you who have to work double shifts or rotations that require you to work around the clock. It's crazy-tough on the body.

As I looked at my day, I first blocked out the usual time for sleep. For argument's sake, let's assume a healthy seven to eight hours. Let's also put that sleep time where "normal" society believes we should sleep: between ten at night and seven in the morning. You can adjust it an hour or so within those parameters.

That leaves us with fifteen to sixteen hours of "awake time" to do with as we please. But wait; most of us need ten hours for work and work-related activities such as commuting. Ten hours. That's a lot of time! We'll get back to work time in a moment. Now, what's left in our day? We have five to seven hours of "me" time, family time, social time, and/or "build-a-better-life" time.

Let's look at each block.

The Sleep Block. Do you feel rested when you wake after a regular night's sleep? How many times do you hit the snooze bar before you get out of bed? A good night's sleep is vital to your health and productivity. It's important to have a bedtime ritual and a morning ritual. These rituals will enhance your sleep quality as they program your subconscious mind to work for you while you sleep.

Start your bedtime ritual about thirty minutes before bed. Turn off the TV. Please don't watch the late news before you go to sleep. Yes, I'm going to be hard on you about your bedtime distractions. The news is broadcast at specific times for a reason. You are susceptible to lower energy frequencies during those hours. But you can take advantage of this lower energy and put some positive programming to work instead. Read a positive book or listen to a CD that inspires and empowers you. Then, do positive affirmations for two to five minutes. Let your energy be high and on purpose when you do this.

Nighttime affirmations allow the energy and feelings within them to sink into your subconscious mind as you sleep. Here's a sample affirmation: "As I sleep, the ideas and concepts of my master plan will become available to me." This time is also good for visualization because positive mental images can help you relax and drift off to sleep. Just before you close your eyes, put a question or challenge out to the Universe for your subconscious mind to work on as you sleep. This bedtime ritual has worked wonders for me. Also, I look at my vision board for a few minutes each night.

Always keep a glass of fresh water on your nightstand. If you wake during the night, you might be thirsty, since sleep can cause mild dehydration. But if you're like me, you'll be too tired, cozy, or lazy to get out of bed and get a glass of water. The internal struggle for sleep vs. quenching your thirst can rob the quality of your sleep.

Once you've established a bedtime ritual, you'll sleep better.

The Morning Block. Next, the morning comes. Morning can be the best part of your day. When you say there isn't enough time in the day to get everything done, I say, "Bullshit!" I'll admit, I'm a morning person. I love my morning time, but not if it's still dark outside. However, I found power in embracing the morning. Do you want to know where to find extra time? Well, it's been there all along—in the morning!

I challenge you to get up one hour earlier than you normally do during the week. Yes, one hour earlier. I know it will be tough for many of you, especially if you already get up at six o'clock in the morning, but hear me out on this one. Set your clock for five o'clock in the morning. Scary, right? Not really, if you shift your awareness of time. While you're changing focus, you might want to change the way you think about the sound your clock emits to help you wake in the morning. Zig Ziglar calls it an "opportunity" clock, not an "alarm" clock. Here's his rationale:

> In society today, we tend to accentuate the negatives instead of the positives. One example is the 'alarm clock' we use to wake ourselves up in the morning. Realistically, when we hear an alarm it generates fear or anxiety. When somebody robs a bank, an alarm is sounded; when there's a fire, someone sounds an alarm. Perhaps waking up to an 'alarm' helps explain the profusion of negative words we use. If you rethink the issue of your clock, you will realize that it is really giving you an *opportunity*. When you hear it ring, you have the opportunity to get up and go. A whole day full of possibilities is available to you once you hear your 'opportunity' clock.

So set your "opportunity" clock for an hour earlier than usual. Don't be afraid. Yes, you need to rest, and you should, for seven or eight hours. However, give yourself the gift of what that extra hour could give you.

Can you recall a day when you had to be at the airport at five in the morning to catch a flight to start an exciting vacation? You know, that time you found yourself packing your bags at midnight, and got only three hours' sleep before it was time to wake up. The clock went off, and *bam,* you were ready and in the car in no time. You even had some lively conversations with your fellow travelers in the boarding area. Not one of you seemed to be suffering from sleep deprivation, right?

It is all in the head! If it's feasible, go to bed thirty minutes earlier. You may need to sacrifice or record your favorite TV show, but if you truly want to be Remarkable, turn off the television. None of the people you respect and admire waste time watching TV. They're too busy making things happen.

Now, with a new wake-up time set on your clock, you have to be ready and willing to wake up at that appointed time. There is a powerful reason for doing this, which I will get to in a moment.

So what should you do with the hour you've created for yourself? It's *your* hour. No one else's. Let the family sleep. This is when you can do what you've been putting off. Go to the gym, write that book, blog, or ezine. Plan your day, watch your children sleep, or build on your hobby. You can also get in an early-morning walk or run. A unique energy exists in the day's early-morning hours. Introduce yourself to the early-morning people in your community. I guarantee you will feel a sense of pride when you acknowledge those runners on the street. They got the same message at some point. Early-morning people are doers! They have big visions, big ideas.

The biggest reason for getting up early is to give yourself your first victory of the day. When you've done this, you just can't help but feel a sense of accomplishment. This feeling sets up your day beautifully because you have a victory under your belt before the day really gets rolling. Later, your family will get up and the world will awaken, but you...you're already way out in front of the daily race. While others are yawning and wiping their eyes, you have done your run, finished that report, listened to an audio program, meditated, taken a hot yoga class, and so on. Also, you'll grow to appreciate just how long each day is and how much actual time you have to be productive.

The Work Block. Whether you're an employee, an entrepreneur, or both, the work block is your biggest energy exchange. How you use this time will dictate a large percentage of your experiences, freedom, and challenges.

It's hard for me to remember what stole and wasted our time before we had social media. Gossip around the water cooler and surfing the Internet were big. However, with the advent of smartphones and social media, all bets are off when it comes to distractions. There are so many shiny little objects vying for your attention, and you know which ones are your biggest time-stealers.

Set up your work block for as much efficiency as possible. You'll need to use some imagination here since I can't describe your unique business environment and the distractions (if any) you may be dealing with. Let's say you're a financial planner. In order to achieve success in your day, you'll need to complete a number of activities, including prospecting, appointments, and follow-ups. Ask yourself, "What are my money-making activities? What decisions and actions can I make in the moment that are part of those money-making activities?" From there, focus on achieving the results you desire. Get your email and social media time out of the way early, and don't spend more than thirty minutes doing it. If you're an online marketer or social media expert, then obviously, the rule doesn't apply. Just make sure you're working rather than socializing.

Put all your peeps on notice that you only respond to emails and social media notices during a set time. Once your inner circle knows you've established these boundaries, they'll back off and won't feel put out if you don't respond to them right away. I know it's hard to refrain from reaching for your cell phone to see who's texted you the latest joke or photo, but don't succumb to temptation. Turn off your "notifiers" if you must. If what you're doing isn't a money-making activity, it's a waste of time.

If you block out specific time for certain activities, you'll soon realize the magic of time management. If you block off two hours for prospecting, use a single process such as phone calls or email. Engage in an activity that involves a singular motion. Don't clutter up your money-making time with a few calls, then a few emails, then some thank-you notes, and then some more phone calls. Make your phone calls for the entire day during a single motion and block of time. Handle your correspondence this way too. Same for your appointments, if possible. By focusing this way, time seems to slow down and you will accomplish much more. Add that to your early morning victory, and it's likely that you've had a stellar day thus far!

Your day is unique to you, and you have to allow for things that are hard to predict or plan. However, by putting the proper parameters in place, you can be Remarkable with your work like never before.

Keeping your energy high will be a challenge, especially since you're getting up one hour earlier. If you don't respect your sugar and hydration levels, you could experience a mid-morning or mid-day crash that will take you out of your money-making rhythm, your effectiveness. Water, water, water! Drink at least a cup of water every hour, and eat something every two hours. Avoid heavy meals, as that will slow you down, but be sure to eat. And water? Well, that's just common sense, and a venti mocha frappuccino doesn't count! Hydrate!

The Social Block. This time is yours to use as you choose. Most people have kids and their kids' routines, and because of that, they believe it's all but impossible to squeeze time for themselves out of what's left. This is another lie people tell themselves. If you've stuck with your schedule up to this point, you'll probably agree that there's a lot of time in a day. Make your social block work for you, just like the rest of your time, and your entire day will be a victory.

At some point in your evening, you can find a one- or two-hour block of time for yourself (most likely when you're watching your favorite TV shows). Now, I'm not telling you to quit TV cold turkey. I enjoy *CSI* and some other cop/techie shows, but for the most part, I don't watch TV because it was truly zapping my life. Ask yourself how much you've gained as a result of watching three to five hours of TV per day. Don't use TV as a way to escape, a coping mechanism in your life. If watching TV is how you cope, then this book has come to you just in time! You might think to yourself, "Well, I only watch PBS and documentaries, so I'm learning." Watching TV can be a great way to learn. However, what are you doing with the knowledge you gain from watching TV? If it doesn't serve your purpose, then it's a form of escape...and that's okay. Try this: during prime time, turn off the TV and just sit there in the stillness. With the remote in your hand, sitting in your favorite chair, just notice everything around you.

I want you to try turning off the TV so you can answer a question. Which is stronger? Is it your will to continue, put down the remote, and try new options? Or is it the TV, calling you to escape back into the void and zone out? The fact that you are reading this book tells me you are stronger than the remote. So, let's look at some activities you can do during your social block that will move you forward.

Men, this is champion and hero time! This is time to interact with your family, kids, wife, partner, or girlfriend. Get outside or go to a favorite restaurant. If you're alone, get out; go to a coffee shop and read a book. In fact, this is a great time to read up on what will move you forward. Perhaps you'll use this time for a business seminar. Listen to CD's, dance, and laugh. Go to a spot that provides a great view of the sunset. This is time to come alive! There's no reason to wait until the weekend to have fun. And guys, if you're in a relationship and your pattern is to go home, put your feet up, and "unplug" from your busy day in front of the tube because you "deserve it," that's not living and that's not being a Remarkable Man.

What can you do tonight that will shake up your routine and make your day complete? You can find at least two hours to enjoy doing something that will help you become Remarkable. Just don't stay up too late!

With your day complete, don't forget to take thirty minutes before bed for your nighttime routine. At this point, you can reflect on your day of victories and accomplishments. You can be proud of the way you used your day to its fullest. As great as it feels, the hardest part will be finding the determination to do it all over the next day. Will you be Remarkable again? Say, "Yes!"

CHAPTER NINE

UNDERSTAND YOUR POWER

You are within God. God is within you.
— Peace Pilgrim, Spiritual Teacher

I am God.

Read it again.

I am God.

What first entered your mind when you read those words?

Now say it out loud. Go on; try it! "I am God."

Here's a big question for you: Can you say it and mean it?

If you are like most men on the planet, you'll think it's a crazy, sacrilegious, blasphemous, die-a-thousand-deaths kind of statement. But before you judge the statement and wonder why I've included it in this book, allow me to share a story that may put it in a better light for you.

I first heard those words many years ago while watching the TV miniseries *Out on a Limb*, starring Shirley MacLaine. Okay, I know you're rolling your eyes right now, but stay with me on this one. There is a scene in the series where Shirley is on the beach near her Malibu home. Her friend, David (John Heard), shares an exercise that helps us recognize God is within. He gets to a point where he asks her to stand up and declare, "I am God."

Shirley's first reaction is, "David, I can't do that!"

His response is, "See how little you believe in yourself?"

With a little nudging, David succeeds in helping Shirley break free from her limiting beliefs and separation from God. They stand with arms stretched open, face the ocean, and proclaim, "I am God!" They repeat the statement until she feels it with her whole being!

This scene stuck with me and I remember trying the exercise myself. It felt foreign and weird at first, as the religious notion of God was embedded in me as part of my upbringing. However, I gave it a shot and began to "feel" the words I said. An incredible wave of energy enveloped me. My lungs filled with deep and deliberate breaths. It felt as if the words themselves were breathing life into me. It seemed as if the Universe were saying, "Finally…he gets it!" Euphoria began to fill me and giddiness flooded my head. It didn't stop there. "I am God!" started out as wimpish and cautionary, but soon I was proclaiming it with a deep and knowing confidence. "I AM GOD!"

I was breathing deeply, almost with a will not my own. It felt good, damn good! In fact, I kept at it for about five minutes, and I felt another shift in awareness beginning to surface. My ego remained in check while I enjoyed this newfound feeling and knowing. A sense of power I'd never felt came over me.

Then it hit me: "I am God!" I am God?

Oh my! What if I am God? What would God be doing?

Then it seemed silly, as my ego popped in with its so-called logical questions about my "reality." *How could I be God? I mean, really. How could a guy like me actually be the omnipresent, Alpha and Omega, the all-knowing, all-seeing Father of the Universe?* It was just a bit too much to take. Okay, it was *a lot* to take! There I was, in my basement apartment, barely making it in the world, but proclaiming, "I am

God." Really?

I'd be lying if I said it stuck. It didn't stick, and I don't expect it to stick with you either on your first try, second try, or even during the next chapter of your life. Saying, "I am God" doesn't mean you're telling yourself that you're the Father as depicted in many religions. Saying "I am God" is a way for you to connect with God's energy and grace. It is in you, and all around you.

One thing was undeniable when I proclaimed, "I am God." It was a sense of knowing and a feeling of connection to my higher self I'd never experienced.

In order to grasp what I mean, you must let go of the last vestiges of your ego as it pertains to what you think about God. If you are religiously inclined and think I've just insulted all you know and believe, I want to get one thing straight. The divine is in you too! In John 10:30, Jesus says, "I and my Father are one." Then in John 14:12, "Most assuredly, I say to you, if a man believes in me, also shall he do the works that I do; and he shall do greater works than these, because I go to the Father." If you believe that, is it so far off to realize God is not outside us, but truly within us? The power I felt that day wasn't an accident; it was Spirit letting me know I was connecting to true consciousness, all that is.

Wayne Dyer said it well. "If you knew who walked beside you at all times, on the path that you have chosen, you could never experience fear or doubt again."

It's a bit of a mindblower to accept that you are "The Creator" of your reality. Think about that title for a moment. "The Creator." If you subscribe to the idea that God created heaven, earth, and all things in between, and if you believe we are a part of God, is it so far out there to believe you create your life and experiences with God? We are all co-creators! Breathe it in. You'll begin to breathe deeply and purposefully. That's your body's way of allowing you to feel the truth.

Once you get past the limiting notion that you are small, and when saying "I am God" no longer feels silly and foreign, you will feel the power and truth of who and what you are.

This power goes much deeper than your ego's span of control. I'm talking about the vibration of love, truth, and connection. Please don't get carried away by the whole God complex thing. Don't let your ego become part of the equation. As you begin to see everyone, and I mean everyone, as the Divine Spirits we are, you'll experience a humbling and powerful sensation of perfection. It puts things in perspective.

If you're in a public place, look at the people around you. See them through new eyes. See them as your "I am God" eyes would see them. But see "I am God" in them too! Each of us is "co-creating" our world. If you are an agnostic or atheist, then perhaps see this statement as Universal energy, flow, or natural perfection. It's imperative that you understand who and what you really are.

Guys, I know it's not easy to comprehend this whole "God Power" thing. Many of you are struggling just as I did. It can be hard to fathom that you are more powerful than anything you could ever imagine. You may be thinking, "Well, if I am God, I wouldn't have put myself through the drama, pain, and suffering I've experienced in life."

I can relate to that because I've had the same thought many times. As I said before, I didn't lock in the "I am" concept when I first heard it. No, I went back to playing the victim again. I did not find myself worthy of being part of such a large concept. Let me save you years of needless suffering and feeling like a victim. If you can get this concept now, then the lessons that follow will be more profound and impactful, and your life will begin to change with rapid certainty.

If you struggle with the idea that you and the Creator are as one, then perhaps you can dial it down to a modicum of acceptance. At least be open to the thought that it *might* be possible to be more than you are. Somewhere deep within you, these words are hitting home—and you know it.

Science backs up your divinity. Quantum science is the blending of science and spirituality because it goes into an area of wonder and perfection. You are made up of about 300 trillion cells. Each cell has about .70 millivolts of stored electrical energy. Multiply that by a few trillion (there's that word again), and you have the potential to create more than 250,000 volts of electricity. So saying you are limited, weak, and powerless is actually a lie. You have the power to create your world as you see fit. Miracles happen when you tap into your God self.

Some of you might be envisioning a character like the sinister Darth Sidious, who turned Anakin Skywalker into Darth Vader in the *Star Wars* movie series. I'm not referring to that kind of power. However, many New Thought scientists believe we have the potential. But that's another story. Let's stay with the Star Wars theme for a moment, and more specifically, with Jedi spiritualism. Here we find a great example of art imitating life. It gives some credence to the idea that we're more than what we believe we are. In *Star Wars*, only a few Jedi knights exist throughout the galaxy. This scenario is a great metaphor for society. Of the more than six billion people on earth, only a few will move into their God power and believe they are infinitely more than they are experiencing in the moment.

The Jedi learn to open their minds, trust their inner feelings, and "Use the Force." To bring this home, there's a force in everything; it permeates the in-between spaces of all that is. It is the space between molecular structures at the quantum level.

Now, before I don my lab coat and pocket protector and get all scientific on you, I need to give you some background. I was fascinated when I first learned about the concept of science and spiritual connections in life, but I had a hard time understanding what it all meant. So I am going to do my best to honor you if you are just scratching the surface on your journey of discovery. And to you who are well-versed in spiritual and scientific matters, I tip my hat and hope this discussion will have you nodding your head in that quiet, all-knowing sort of way.

Have you ever been to an area of a city, typically out near the edges, where suburbs seem to pop up everywhere? You may see a freeway, bridge, or interchange under construction. It's a huge project, and they're adding many lanes of highway. In some cases, you may be driving on a different part of the road, where only two lanes are being used and the other six are barricaded, not a single car on them! You may have even seen off-ramps and bridges leading to nowhere! You might think to yourself, "This is ridiculous. They're spending all this money on a huge project we'll hardly use. What a waste of taxpayers' money!"

The truth is that city planners plan for the density and growth of a population. They meticulously calculate future traffic usage. With that data, they move forward with projects to meet projected growth or expand when needed. That way, inflation takes less of a toll later on, rather than reverse engineering after the fact. That's the theory, anyway. Just like in that '80s song by The Fixx, "It doesn't mean much now. It's built for the future."

The point I am trying to make here is that something else is overbuilt for its time. It's a complex machine, functioning at perhaps 10 percent of its capability. It is a machine built for the future. What is this incredible machine? It's you! It's the human body.

Now, before the neurologists call "Foul," read on. I'm referring to the new science that points to an exciting future. More people in the scientific world are waking up to the idea that we've only scratched the surface of our potential. Experts estimate that your body currently only uses 10 percent, at best, of what it has available. Amazing, right? Your brain, both left and right hemispheres, is firing at a small fraction of its potential.

Let me give you an illustration to explain what I mean. Imagine getting a new pick-up truck. You know the type—the invincible, mammoth vehicle pulling heavy equipment through the mud at a construction site, with a tough baritone voice in the background raving about the truck's huge payload and towing capabilities. Yeah, that truck. Now imagine that truck hauling a full load of foam "popcorn." The truck is full and 100 percent involved in hauling foam from point A to point B, right? However, would you agree that the truck isn't even using a fraction of its potential power? Of course it's not. The truck is hauling light-as-a-feather foam! Now, take the same truck and payload capacity. But this time, imagine it's your life, complete with everything you've experienced—good and bad. Easy-breezy up to this point, right? It's all the brainpower you've ever needed, so no big deal. Now, imagine you have the big powerful truck with the light and fluffy cargo we call life. Then imagine discovering there are four more gears and a couple of things called torque and horsepower—things you never knew about. Your brain is just like that truck, full of potential, but not fully engaged.

Let's move on to your eyes. The rods and cones in your eyes only see 10 percent of the light spectrum (visible light), yet they are receptive to seeing much more. The challenge again is your brain's ability to interpret visual impulses. Your ability to see is confined to reflective light. However, there's more going on just beyond your visual perception. According to a definition from the International College of Medicine and Healing, vibrational frequency is "the rate at which the atoms and sub particles of a being or object vibrate. The higher this vibrational frequency, the closer it is to the frequency of Light."

Vibrational frequencies can be tuned into or tuned out, depending on your own vibrational resonance. For example, do you recall a time when you were on a busy street or in a shopping mall and a friend was waving and calling your name, but you neither saw nor heard him? You would have walked right by him if he hadn't tapped you on the shoulder and said, "Hello." Your friend says, "Hey, I was calling you. When I waved, you were looking right at me, but you didn't see me!"

You almost missed this encounter, but it wasn't because you were being rude or ignoring your friend. It happened because he wasn't in a vibrational frequency for you to see him. He was hiding in plain sight, if you will. As your frequency rises, your "sight" will change dramatically.

Within your DNA is a double helix of incredible life-giving data. Yet there are unused, or "dormant," codes within the DNA. Not only that, we have the coding for a twelve-strand DNA helix. Scientists call this the "junk" or "shadow" DNA. This "junk" actually holds the key to a higher awareness of your emotional, mental, and spiritual body.

Why do we use so little of our potential? What does it all mean? Well, I agree with many people around the world who believe that something profound is about to take place, something that could trigger a cascade effect and "fire up" our DNA. This DNA time code has been dormant, waiting for the signal. This idea may sound like science fiction, but the science and data creates enough wonder and hope to want to witness this new beginning and chapter of human evolution.

I bring this information to your attention to illustrate a point. I want you to realize just how powerful you are. This reality is more than we imagine when we think about a man with power. An awakening is occurring. You know it and can feel it. You know it because it's already in your DNA! Like a bird that needs to fly south in the fall, or the caterpillar that instinctively needs to build a chrysalis to transform, you *know* something is happening. Your desire to be a

Remarkable Man is preparing you for something more. If you believe that you have the potential to accomplish so much more, then the possibilities are endless. You are not just your physical and mental self; you are a part of the Universal intelligence.

With this new way of looking at who you really are, might it be possible to reassess your challenges, pains, and shortcomings? Might this new vision be a great way to see others? Acquiring this vision allows you to move forward, bust through your limiting self, and be Remarkable in your life. From here, you can put things in perspective. Most of our lives are filled with lessons we need to experience in order to learn, course-correct, and remember what we have forgotten: who we truly are.

In the next section, we'll go into essentials for living the life you want to live. We'll examine how to be champions to women, heroes to children, and brothers to each other. With your mind opened a little more, or perhaps blown wide open, you are now ready to learn about your Remarkable Man within. The Remarkable Man project is part of your wake-up call. It's a way to help shorten the learning curve so you can live the life you want to live!

The essentials that follow are critical, not only for living a better life, but also for living the life you, a Remarkable Man, want to live. You must begin to take a more active role in your life as your consciousness increases. Your natural gifts and talents will call you with greater intensity. If you are not already engaged in that which you're called to achieve, then think about what achieving your vision will do for your life. I'm not saying to quit your current job, leave your relationship, or make a sudden 180-degree turn if you are not happy. Although that may be what's needed. I'm just saying to get ready for a shift. Life has a way of dealing you a hand or two you may not be prepared for, but the Universe knows you can handle it. These synchronistic events will take you where you need to go. Being a Remarkable Man means being ready for these "shake-up" moments before they happen.

The next part of this book walks you through **The Seven Essentials** of what it takes to be a Remarkable Man.

PART THREE

THE SEVEN ESSENTIALS

ESSENTIAL #1

SELF-RESPONSIBILITY

Now if you know what you're worth, then go out and get what you're worth. But ya gotta be willing to take the hits, and not pointing fingers saying you ain't where you wanna be because of him, or her, or anybody! Cowards do that and that ain't you! You're better than that!
— Rocky Balboa, *Rocky*

Self-responsibility leads off our essentials list because being a Remarkable Man means taking control of your life. To have proper control, you must detach from the actions and circumstance of others and focus only on your own activities and thoughts. Taking full responsibility for your life is one of the most liberating gifts you can give yourself. However, it isn't easy. You see, a little thing called ego gets in the way every now and then. As I mentioned earlier, I am going to push your ego to its uncomfortable limits here.

I know you realize self-responsibility is important and a rather obvious component of life. You've read and heard about self-responsibility from great authors, speakers, and leaders. However, nothing gets more lip service than that of self-responsibility. You can know about it and live it to a point, or scratch the surface of what your ego will allow, but you'll need courage if you want to dive into the truth. Courage you have yet to use fully. So my question for you is: Are you ready?

You are 100 percent responsible for your life! Yes, 100 percent responsible. This responsibility includes your debts, failed relationships, health issues, hurt, pain, suffering...all of it! There is no blaming your parents, your heredity, your partner, your children, or your environment.

How's your ego holding up? I can already hear the "Yeah, buts" going.

"Yeah, but my situation is different. That guy cut me off on the road and I went into the ditch," you say. "I'm gonna be in pain for the rest of my life."

Or..."Yeah, but my dad was an alcoholic. That's why I am messed up!"

Or..."Yeah, but I was abused as a child and was robbed of my innocence. The pain in my life is not my fault."

Or..."Yeah, but she nags me all day long. I just can't take it anymore."

I could probably fill a book with "Yeah, but" stories. They are real and convincing stories for you. They are the stories you have hung onto to justify, or escape from, your life experiences. Did you catch that part about them being *your* stories? They're the stories you tell people, the movies you choose to replay, to give your life a sense of meaning. These are your way to justify and make excuses that keep you where you are.

If you are reeling from the idea that you created your trauma, hardship, and drama, you are not alone. I feel and understand your resistance. I probably had more difficulty grasping the concept of self-responsibility than most. My ego was so entrenched in the idea that my failures were due to external sources that the mere mention of another idea would get me angry or agitated inside. That is where I began to fight for my limitations. Oh, and fight I did. My sister constantly asked me to *try* to see where I could have created my situation. No chance. Even with my awareness and knowledge of the law of attraction, I still had a story, an excuse. You see, the ego hates to be wrong. Now, before those of you who say, "There's no right or wrong, only perfection" get upset, I get you and agree with that theory—to an extent. Unfortunately, as you should understand by now, the ego does not play in that world. The ego is stuck on right and wrong, day and night.

Let's explore some areas where we typically chalk up our experiences to events on the outside.

"I was in a car accident." Someone hit you. It was completely out of your hands. You were just sitting there, and *wham,* A car hit you from behind. "It wasn't my fault!"

I'll agree; the accident wasn't your fault on the physical plane. However, you created the experience. Yes, you did! You created it through your energy patterns. No, this is not crazy talk. It's the truth. Your higher self knows how you are vibrating, and it will give you experiences to support that pattern. Look at the accident from a higher perspective. What events preceded and followed the accident? Who came into your life as a result? Who got upset? Who played the victim? Who won a settlement? Who lost? Indeed, there was a collision, no argument there, but there was no accident! You manifested the experience for a new level of awareness, appreciation, and understanding.

Can you remember a time when you were having a crappy day and it seemed like no matter what you did, you just got dumped on even more? Now consider the thoughts that go with a crappy day...they're crappy thoughts. Like attracts like! What you experience in life is ultimately due to the energy and thoughts you give out. You attract what you put into the Universe.

"A loved one died." This event is one of the most tragic and heartbreaking of all human events. If you are dealing with this experience,

please know that I have walked in your shoes. I feel your pain if this loss is fresh and raw to you. By no means do I want to diminish or belittle the hurt created when a loved one dies.

The people we manifest come to us for a reason, a season, or a lifetime. Most people are in the "reason" category; they're in and out of our lives to provide a brief experience or introduce us to others. They play a significant role in our lives as direction turners, angels, and guides.

In the "season" category are those who play a long-term role such as lifelong friends, colleagues, and significant relationships. The lessons these people provide are deeper and more profound. They support your vibrational frequency.

Finally, there is the "lifetime" category. This group will play the most significant role in your life. These are family members or soul mates. They can span two or three generations in front of you and behind you. These people teach and shape you, regardless of age or where they are in your life. You can try to ignore them if you think that's best, but know they are connected to you, no matter what you do to escape or deny it. These people are your greatest source of learning and life lessons.

The level at which a death impacts your life correlates with where the person fits in. Death of a person in the "reason" category typically triggers surprise, sadness, disappointment, regret, and reflection. The mourning process is relatively short. The death of someone in the "season" category triggers deep feelings of loss and personal impact. Chances are many in your peer group are effected as well, which creates a greater energy of sadness, loss, and pain.

Death of a person in the "lifetime" category is so personal and deep that it causes all the hurt and suffering of a lifetime to surface. When we suffer this kind of loss, we experience a realm of feelings—regret, victimization, anger, rage, revenge, loneliness, abandonment, trauma, resentment, relief, forgiveness, acceptance, freedom, and sorrow.

What is the role of self-responsibility when your loved one dies? You remain responsible for your experiences, even the loss of a loved one. Breathe that in for a moment before you judge it. You, as did many others, manifested the loss of someone close to you. However, you only manifested the way you experienced it. As difficult as it is, the death of someone close to you is a lesson for you and everyone who cared about that person.

My parents had similar experiences when both of my grandmothers passed on. My grandmothers were two different women. Yet what the families experienced after each funeral was strikingly familiar. Each family member mourned the loss in his or her own way, but when it came to dividing the assets, the siblings (my aunts and uncles) were at each other's throats over who'd get what. The death of their mother was lost on some of them. However, it brought them together from all over the country to face each other, rather than ignoring each other as they'd done for many years. They were forced to get real and deal with the issues buried deep within each of them. Cooler heads eventually prevailed and some true healing was evident. This healing paved the way for family members to forgive and let go, to love and respect one another. It gave some of the older family members, and those who were sick, permission to go home too. This permission was what their souls were seeking, and the catalyst had to be the passing of my grandmothers.

The death of someone you love, as painful and tragic as it is in the moment, teaches you something powerful. You created the experience for a much bigger reason than you realize in the moment. And as time goes by, you will begin to understand why that soul had to leave, why he or she was called home. You aren't responsible for the person's passing (unless a law was broken and the courts ruled differently). There was a covenant between your loved one and the Universe, and you had nothing to do with it. You're only responsible for how you respond to it. Self-responsibility in these situations will help you come to terms with the loss, and the lessons will come with more insight, understanding, and compassion.

Obviously, the death of a loved one comes with profound meaning, more than the space I can afford it here. Just remember that everything is designed for perfection, and the most powerful lessons and gifts can be found here if you are open and ready to accept them.

"My partner cheated on me." Oh, this is a tough one to take responsibility for. I mean really, how could you possibly take responsibility for something someone else did? Your friends might even say, "Dude, you were the victim here. I mean, come on! There's no way you're responsible for this." Right?

Wrong. You are responsible for all of it. When I say all of it, I mean *all of it*! Not 99 percent, not 99.5 percent. I mean 100 percent of it! You are responsible for your part of the experience. You drew the drama leading up to the "event" into your life. At a subconscious level, you manifested the experience to learn and grow from it.

Now, with your ego fully present, I'm sure you think I'm off my rocker on this one. What could possibly be the lesson?

Perhaps some of you have experienced this situation with other partners in your life. Maybe it isn't a one-time experience for you. If you've experienced infidelity before, or if you're experiencing the pain for the first time, you've drawn it into your life for a reason. Until you truly get that, you will continue to manifest the experience.

What part of you, what self, pushes people away from you? What role do you play in giving and receiving of intimacy? When it comes to heartfelt, meaningful relationships, a myriad of energies come to the surface, energies that either attract or repel your partner. If a partner is seeking the love and affection of another while still in a relationship with you, know that it was not an overnight decision.

In most cases, affairs are the product of a long-term absence of connection and affection. You withdrew, shut down, gave up, dropped your authentic masculine power, let yourself go, stopped caring, or took the relationship for granted. The reason doesn't really matter; what matters is that you understand your behavior patterns and take responsibility for them. You created the circumstances in your life. Perhaps you did so to end a relationship that was not serving you, to set yourself free to be on your own, to travel, or to connect with old and new friends. Perhaps your true love was waiting in the wings of your future, but couldn't come into your life until this relationship ended.

Sometimes the Universe will create the cheating to make it easier for you to dump the person. You might be a great guy in love with someone less than ideal for you. Others may see it and try to warn you, only to have you get upset, discount their warnings, and continue in your delusion that your partner is "all that!" When you catch her or him cheating, it's like the Universe had to pull out the big guns to get you back on track. It's a sign that you need to move on. Remember: The Universe won't give you anything you can't handle.

Guys, I would be remiss if I didn't put the cheater's shoe on the other foot for a moment. Self-responsibility includes your side of the relationship too. If you are cheating on your wife, partner, or girlfriend, or if you are thinking about it, hold up! I mean, WTF? If you have the balls to sleep around, but don't have the balls to talk to your significant other about how your needs aren't being met, how the hell can I get you to be a Remarkable Man?

Huddle up! I feel like a coach who's pissed off at his star player for screwing up!

Fellas, if you're cheating, I need to shake some sense into you. You're better than that. If you think a one-night stand or a secret liaison on a business trip to Cincinnati won't be a big deal, then you have no idea what an authentic relationship is. Love is an action word and you have to work at it. Self-responsibility means taking a higher road.

All relationships, no matter how long or short, have two wonderful souls at their core. Both of you went into this arrangement with incredible odds against you, but you found each other, and for some reason, you fell in love. Perhaps you have children too.

Both of you deserve to have the other know what's going on in your head and heart. If you're not "getting any," and you feel like cheating to get your rocks off...stop! For example, say you're not getting the love or nurturing you feel you deserve at home. You're thinking the girl from the coffee supply company is always friendly and seems to "get" you, and you're texting her about possibly getting together. Stop!

Guys, I could go on and on about scenarios where a guy might be tempted or actually cheat. Hear me out. If you are not getting your needs met in any area of your relationship, if you haven't expressed it, or if you've had several "talks" about it and still cheat...you are a huge wuss! Yes, that's right! A wuss! A Nancy boy!

Why am I calling you out like this? I'll tell you. You have a responsibility to your partner to put your feelings and challenges on the table. Be honest. You're a man, for crying out loud! Act like one! Tell your partner exactly how you feel. Most infidelity is due to a failure to communicate. If you've exhausted your ability to express your unhappiness in the relationship and nothing changes, what should you do?

Let me rephrase that. What should the Remarkable Man do? Pack your bags! You're done. Leave the relationship. Your partner does not deserve to be dishonored by you cheating. You have a responsibility to your partner, children, and yourself to be the best man you can be.

Beautiful women will tempt you and come into your life at "just the right time" when you've got game and she flashes that smile. Yeah, you know the one. You can chat her up, flirt a little, but ask yourself, "Where am I taking this? What do I need out of this? Do I need to prove I've still got it? How far does it go?"

Being Remarkable means loving and knowing yourself enough to know you don't need someone on the outside to validate how great you are. Check into the girl who's waiting for you at home, my friend. If she loves you, she will listen and want to make changes. And be open to make some changes of your own if you truly love her too. That's a Remarkable Man!

When it comes to self-responsibility, I could fill volume after volume of books with examples, but the point is that in order to be a Remarkable Man, you must take full responsibility for your experiences and how you participate in the movie of your life.

This isn't an easy process. It takes time to grasp the power and significance that self-responsibility can have in your life. It took me an embarrassingly long time to understand self-responsibility. I gave it lip service and owned it only when it made me look good or gave me a fleeting sense of personal power. However, the true essence of self-responsibility comes only when you are truly ready. The experience is so liberating, so fantastically rich and freeing, that I can't put it into words.

To me, self-responsibility was like reading a book five times before truly understanding the message. Or like looking at a 3-D picture puzzle...you stare and stare at it, but the crazy image only gives you a headache. People laugh with joy and discovery when they finally see the dolphin jumping (or whatever it is), but even though you squint and strain, you just can't make the image come to you. Eventually, in a moment of relaxed gazing, it jumps at you! Just briefly, your brain interpreted your optic messages a little differently. You shout excitedly, "There! I saw…." Then it is gone, but you know it was there, if only for a second. You try again, looking in the general direction of the image. Then, as if by magic, it slowly moves toward you. You take a deep breath as the sensation of seeing something from nothing gives you a rush. "The dolphin! I see it now!" Not just once, either. After that, every time you see the 3-D swirls and patterns, you can pull the hidden images out at will. It's easy, as you are now wired for the experience.

Self-responsibility is similar. You have to work at it, be present, and know that you are at the right place at the right time, successfully engaged in the right activity...always!

ESSENTIAL #2

THE COMPANY YOU KEEP

We are the sum total of the five people we spend the most time with.
— Jim Rohn

Being a Remarkable Man in your life and in the lives of those you care about is what you are ultimately after, or you wouldn't have chosen to read this book. If you are to show up, you must take a hard look not only at yourself, but at the people with whom you associate. In the previous chapter, I mentioned that people come into our lives for a reason, a season, or a lifetime. It's usually up to you to decide where people will fit in. It's also up to you to learn and understand the gifts and messages they have for you. In other words, discover what they're here to teach you.

No matter what your station in life, you have manifested a diverse group of friends, family, and acquaintances. If you were to take an inventory of the people you've become friends with over your life, what would be one common personality trait? How does each person lift you up and move you forward?

The people you attract play a key role in molding and shaping the man you become. Most often, our friends and family members represent a comfort zone, a familiarity, and a fall-back position. You know they'll accept you no matter what happens. I mean, that's the mark of a good friend and loving family member, right? They'll catch you if you fall, help you up when you stumble, or perhaps keep your feet planted on the ground. Sadly, few people grow up with family members and friends who champion their dreams, goals, and desires.

My parents did the best they could with what they knew. They were simple folks with simple values. I recall having a very loving family during the first eight years of my life. We did not suffer for much, and as a family of four, our needs were met. My sister was happy with her Barbie Doll collection, and I had my model trains and Hot Wheels toy cars and trucks. We usually found what we wanted for Christmas under the tree.

Compare that to the family that moved in next door when I was three. Larry became my best friend, but his family was unique and a bit odd to my simple eyes. His father was a shop manager for the railway, and his mother was a nurse. His grandparents lived a block away. Larry and his brother spent weekends on the family boat. They made weekly trips to the town library. The only library I knew about was the one in my school. Larry and Glen, his brother, were involved in sports such as soccer, baseball, swimming, and skiing. I didn't envy their life; in fact, I never really noticed the difference—except when I had dinner at their place. They always started with a salad, which I thought was weird, and Larry's parents always had a glass of wine with dinner. As time went on, I realized his parents were worldly and well travelled. They were sports enthusiasts themselves; they skied all winter, biked, and went deep-sea fishing in the summer. They were involved in the community too. They transferred this zest for life to their boys, and it showed. They knew things about the world I did not know or care to know. I never understood why they were so much more exuberant, outgoing, and smarter.

As much as Larry and I were friends and lived next door to each other, our parents did not associate with each other very much. They were friends, but weren't close friends. As I grew older, I realized there was a class system right on my block! But as a child, I didn't see it. As I grew up, my dad's career advanced, and the class lines dissolved. I'd lost touch with my childhood friends by the time I was sixteen, but I learned later in life that Larry and Glen have travelled the world extensively and enjoyed successful careers.

The reason I bring up the contrast in families is to illustrate how our families and the experiences we are exposed to shape us from an early age. Again, my parents did the best they could with what they knew. However, my shyness, low self-esteem, and lack of confidence were products of my environment in those early years. My parents argued over money issues. I remember their shouting matches and the lack of respect they seemed to have for each other's station in life. Neither was proud of the other, and they resented each other for where they found themselves. Since they didn't understand they were on a journey together, the wounds wouldn't heal.

That was a long time ago, and my parents have grown and evolved tremendously since then. They divorced just after I left for college. Their journey took many twists and they are good friends now. I am both proud and humbled by the sacrifices they made to give my sister and me the best upbringing they could afford and offer.

The company you keep at an early stage shapes and molds your character to a great degree. As you get older, your parents' influence wanes and makes way for your peers to influence you. The friends you manifest throughout life play a great role in your journey. I'm not discounting the impact of siblings or extended family members. They're usually there throughout your life, so you have to understand the role they played or are playing now.

I like the following analogy, "Crabs In A Bucket," because it brings home the impact of the company you keep.

If you take one crab and put it in a bucket, it will eventually escape. However, if you put two crabs in a bucket, they will most likely die there. The reason? As they try to escape, one grabs the other's legs, and they pull each other down. This behavior goes on and on until they have no strength left, and die. They're not acting on a "Me First" or "Oh no, you don't" impulse; they do it unconsciously, grasping at whatever they can to get a leg up (pardon the pun) and survive.

Are there any crabs in your bucket? Is there someone in your life right now who doesn't support you, someone who's dragging you down? How often have you had a great idea, vision, or business opportunity, only to have people pull you back down to their level—back into the bucket? It happens all the time, and it can stop a dream in its tracks.

People look for acceptance and belonging in many ways. Dream stealers know this and frequently play the selfish card. They act based on their sense of insecurity. They know, maybe only subconsciously, that if you become a success, you probably won't have a place in your life for them. Your success will also be a catalyst for them to do some self-exploration as to why they aren't successful. They won't like doing this reflection; they try to avoid it. It's easier to dash your hopes and dreams instead.

Now back to my earlier question. Are there any crabs in your bucket? This might be the first time you've ever wondered about the impact people have in your life. A lot of insight and self-awareness occurs when you truly do an inventory of the people you attract and associate with. So, I want you to do *just that*. Take an inventory of the five most influential people currently in your life.

Take out a piece of paper or your journal and write down the names of these five people, and leave about five lines between each one. Next, for each person, list five qualities you admire. Once you have your list of all five people and their five admirable qualities, go back, and see which qualities each person shares. Put a "1" next to the quality that appears most often. Put a "2" next to the quality that comes up next, then a "3," and so on.

Here's an example for you to "score."

1. SHELLY

    a. Smart

    b. Funny

    c. Giving

    d. Loving

    e. Stylish

2. TANYA

    a. Trusting

    b. Loyal

    c. Giving

    d. Creative

    e. Adventurous

3. PAUL

    a. Talented

    b. Giving

    c. Smart

    d. Hard worker

    e. Creative

4. TREVOR

    a. Big heart

    b. Loyal

    c. Driven

  d. Honest

  e. Courageous

5. TYRELL

  a. Giving

  b. Generous

  c. Hard worker

  d. Original

  e. Fun

This exercise allows you to understand your connections with the people you have manifested in your life. Every aspect of a person's personality is a mirror of your own. If you dislike certain parts of a person's character, please realize he or she is simply reflecting parts of you that you don't want to acknowledge.

It's true; birds of a feather flock together. If you want to reach a new level in life, and most Remarkable Men do, ask yourself, "Where do people at that level hang out?" Do they go to the pub on the corner and watch football every Monday night? Do they watch bowling on TV in the mid-afternoon? I highly doubt it. We tend to associate with people within our own economic level. Yes, you might have one friend who's very successful, and you might have one who's always in a struggle. But they cancel each other out for the common de-nominator...you! You're in the middle. You have all the traits of both friends. There's your lazy self, your action self, your victim self, and your champion self—and they're all vying for your attention. The question is, which ones truly serve you and move you forward?

One of the most difficult things to do in life is to let go of the people who limit our growth (the crabs in our bucket). When you take a stand for who you truly are and decide you're no longer going to settle for anything less than the best in people, your life changes for the better.

Many men endure years of heartache, loneliness, and codependency because they're afraid to leave a relationship that has lost its purpose. The people who come into your life—be it for a reason, a season, or a lifetime—represent the lessons you've manifested. Each person you interact with and befriend becomes a conduit for learning. However, many of us don't know how to spot the signs that the learning has ended and the universal contract is over. Rather, we seek to blame, feel we've done something wrong, or project an aspect of ourselves that neither of us in the relationship signed up for. So here are a few tips to assist you in making one of the hardest decisions of your life.

1. Does the person make you a priority in his or her life, or are you an option?

2. Do you feel angst, frustration, or uneasiness around that person?

3. Does the person support and applaud your dreams and goals?

4. Do you feel alive and a better person when you are around him or her?

5. How much of your true self do you have to give up to be with him or her?

As much as it pained me to move out of the house I shared with my ex and her two wonderful girls, I knew, at a higher level, that our contract would never be long-term. Oh yes, I fought that idea. *What if we just worked at it a little more? What if I were more successful? Why doesn't she love me?* My ego self had a field day with the heartache and feelings of loss and separation. The wounds were deep because I thought I was incomplete without her. I'd forgotten who and what I am.

Our breakup wasn't quick. It took time since we were still good friends and confidants. We decided to work on ourselves. She grew tremendously during that time, spiritually and financially. I, on the other hand, stagnated. I was trying in vain to rebuild my company, and I wasn't getting where I wanted to be financially. Slowly, the juice or desire to save what we'd had began to fade. Yes, we remained friends, but I knew she wanted me to reclaim my power, sweep her off her feet, and be the Remarkable Man she'd once known. But alas, only I could make that happen. As much as I wanted things to change, nothing happened. For many months, I had to be patient and do the hard inner work. During that time, I felt us drifting further apart. Her career was taking off and she seemed to be manifesting a wonderful life. This change, too, was a sign that our life contract was done. Although it seemed inexplicable, our lives were playing out exactly as they were meant to. We knew we'd been together for some much-needed and powerful lessons.

If I hadn't fallen from grace, we might have lasted a few more years, but then closing the contract would have been even more difficult. The Universe was perfect in its timing, as it always is. As with many relationships, she was there for a "reason." I'm grateful for the time we spent together, the love we shared, and through her, I met some great people who are still my friends today.

Now it's time for you to look at the relationships in your life that may influence your children (if you have any). Think back to when you were a kid and your father's friends stopped by. What was the atmosphere like then? How did his friends make you feel? I was lucky because my dad's friends were good guys. I called them "Uncle" Bob, "Uncle" Bill, and "Ol' Les." I didn't see them much because Dad kept the home front as a family place. But I remember the good fellows they were; my dad chose well.

The friends you choose easily influence your children. Kids see your friends as "inner circle" people, like family. They think, "If he's one of

Dad's friends, then he must be a nice man." So their guard is lower. Unfortunately, we've all heard stories of what happened when that trust was misplaced or abused, with tragic results.

Choose your friends well, and be mindful of how they behave around your children. Instill a "no tolerance" rule for obscene and abusive language, excessive drinking, or taunting of any kind. For the same reason, if your friends have children, it's your duty to honor all aspects of those friendships, including their families. If you're single, then you know how tough it can be for a family man to go out with the boys. He craves some men-only time, but knows his place. What you can do is amp up your enthusiasm for what he has. Let him know that being a dad and husband is the best thing for him. Engage his kids; ask them questions. Get into their space in a fun and playful way. You already have an "in" with them through their father; don't take that honor and responsibility lightly. Your married friends will appreciate you on a much deeper level because you, their brother, make them feel that they belong with their families.

As a dad, sit down with your children and get them to make a list of their closest friends. Then ask them to tell you what they like about each friend. It's similar to the exercise you just completed. If you can go deeper, ask them to tell you about their friends' families. This exercise will help you understand what's influencing your children outside the family, and give you a mirror of how your children see themselves.

Looking at relationships with a learning attitude empowers you to accept everyone you meet. You'll see the value a person might offer you—and how you might help someone along the way. As you grow, the mirror people hold will reflect an image of yourself that you can feel good about. The Universe puts people in your environment for a reason. These people are the cast of characters you need to complete the movie of your life.

Think about the seemingly impossible circumstances involved with meeting someone new. People come to you through impossible odds. Just like a scene in a romantic movie, you may have passed each other for years and missed each other by seconds. That's because you weren't a vibrational match at the time. Literally, you could not see each other. You weren't meant to meet until you did!

Romantic relationships, friendships, business partnerships, and clients all come to you because of a vibrational match. These are the angels of light and dark, who match your vibrational frequency. If you choose to learn the lessons as you go, the chances of having to repeat them will fall away and you'll manifest people who help you move forward rather than becoming crabs in your bucket.

Recognizing the power of the company you keep is a strong revelation. It will serve you well in discerning who and what you want to have in your Remarkable life.

YOU CREATE YOUR REALITY

Spoon Boy: Do not try to bend the spoon. That's impossible. Instead, only try to realize the truth.

Neo: What truth?
Spoon Boy: There is no spoon.
Neo: There is no spoon?
Spoon Boy: Then you'll see that it is not the spoon that bends; it is only yourself.

— *The Matrix*

In order for me to become Remarkable, I had to get clear on what I truly wanted. I needed to make a commitment to the reality I desired. It wasn't enough for me to lament about the life I didn't want. I was an expert in that area and could manifest negativity all day. *That* was easy! I'd honed my ability to manifest learning experiences that I hated. I was good at it because my ego refused to allow me to learn the lesson...so repeat it, I did!

When I decided to be Remarkable, I had to draw a line in the sand. It wasn't about behaviors that were no longer acceptable; it was about my dominant thoughts. Self-worth and self-esteem are often linked. To be honest, I often thought the two were somewhat the same. However, they're quite different. Understanding the difference between self-worth and self-esteem can make the learning curve easier. Self-worth really has to do with how much you feel you deserve something, or feeling you don't deserve something because you haven't earned it or worked hard enough for it. Self-esteem, on the other hand, is similar to your level of confidence. Your self-esteem can also fluctuate based on superficial judgments by yourself and those around you, often based on performance. Regardless of what level our self-esteem may be at from moment to moment, as men, we all have a high level of self-worth, whether we believe so or not.

My self-esteem was low because I allowed it to be that way. I based much of my self-esteem on what others thought about me. I was in my ego a lot, and when that happens, life becomes a fragile existence. My moods hinged on the praise or value others saw in me. On my path to the bottom, I didn't get many words of praise or value, and my external world reflected it. To support this mindset, I hung around with negative people. My self-worth naturally took a hit and my net worth followed. Thus, my life became a repeating spiral of lack and frustration. A frown replaced my smile. I ended up with permanent creases in my forehead from scowling so much. Who wants to be around a guy like that? Nobody!

To create the reality I wanted, I had to work on both my self-worth and my self-esteem. I needed to understand clearly the nature of self-worth and my self-esteem and how the ego influences them. As with most men, my ego was in the driver's seat most of the time, fighting every step of the way. With my self-awareness, personal growth, and understanding of the Universe and my place in it, I couldn't get past the ego's control over me.

By now, you may have figured out that I view the ego as a villain to avoid or conquer. The ego is like that in a very real way. The ego, which I will discuss in detail in the next chapter, is like your cunning doppelganger, your evil twin, your psychotic dual self. The reality you create will depend on how much you can control your ego.

You create your reality every day. Everything is a vibrational frequency, and you attract the frequencies with which you're most aligned. The challenge is that the vibrations must begin within you. As men, most of us are reactive rather than responsive. We believe in *stimulus first* and *response second*. This situation used to drive me nuts because when I attracted things I didn't want, I'd become angry, frustrated, and depressed. *How can I possibly be attracting this crap? I think I'm doing the work, yet nothing but crap is happening.* Are you with me? Have you felt that way too? Are you experiencing it now?

Well, I am here to tell you that your ego is setting you up to fail. You see, until you get your self-esteem and self-worth in check and pointing in the right direction, you are doomed to keep on repeating the same lower world experiences. To have a truly Remarkable life, you need to feel your God-power, your connection to all that is. This comes from understanding who you are. As mentioned in a previous chapter, you are God. If you struggle with this truth, you'll create separation and duality, which your ego loves to promote.

Your ego says, "How can you be God? I mean, seriously, look at your life! It's all you can do to survive in these trying times. *You are God.* Oh, please! Come down to earth and live in the 'real' world with everybody else. Look, there's your favorite TV show! Grab some beer and nachos, and forget those silly thoughts of grandeur. Tomorrow, you can buy something you don't need, with money you don't have, and hang around with people just like you. You like that, remember?"

The reality you believe in so strongly is an illusion. Just imagine the self-worth you'd have if you understood that you are the Creator. Is it so hard to believe? Since everything in the Universe is energy, and since you're connected to that energy, you're made of the same stuff as everything else. Add some "Big C"—Consciousness—and you join the most powerful beings on earth.

The reality of the Remarkable Man must be the reality you prefer. It's based on your highest ideals. Begin with thoroughly understanding your self-worth. When you visualize your preferred reality, do you sincerely believe you can have it? Or do you view it as a pipe dream? You must wholeheartedly believe in your Remarkable reality and trust that you're worthy of this reality. You must raise your vibration level, and acknowledge your power to manifest what you want. Don't just pay this lip service. You must know it at your very core. Trust and believe in yourself; then trust and believe the Universe will deliver what you want. You must be in exact vibrational match with the reality you want and hold that vibration until your new life unfolds before you. No deviation, doubts, or excuses!

As I've said from the beginning, this work won't be easy. In fact, it will be the most challenging work you will ever do. However, you must *be* what you want before you can *have* what you want. Yeah, I hated this concept. Thanks to my ever-present ego, I fought this idea because it didn't make sense to me. But as I backed myself into a corner with ego statements, I realized I had to take it seriously if I were going to change my life.

> *You do not get what you want, you get what you are.*
> — James Allan

All the law of attraction and ancient philosophy books in my library began to make sense. Be, do, have. Simple! Okay, but not easy. You may have heard about people who experienced overnight miracles in their lives based on these principles. Were these people special? How did they purge their egos, old selves, and lower thoughts so quickly? The common denominator was their firm, unshakable belief in who and what they were.

Any time your ego surfaces and says something negative, immediately cancel it out by reciting a positive affirmation. Affirmations are a powerful way to cause the neuroreceptors in your brain to accept a new program to create the new you. Despite this fact, I found that saying affirmations a few times a day wasn't enough. My ego, doubting self, and negative memories were too strong and came too frequently to allow a new way of thinking to stay in place very long.

I needed to repeat affirmations every chance I could. I said them mostly in my head since I was in public a lot. Saying them repeatedly triggered a corresponding vision of the life I desired. Affirmations raised my feelings of self-worth. I also grabbed onto the Creator self more readily and began to believe in myself. I began to "be" a vibrational match with the reality I wanted to create. For the first time in my life, I got it. The Universe has no choice but to reflect experiences that are in keeping with that vibration.

You'll have to expend some effort to become Remarkable enough to create your reality. But remember, this is your life. Is your life worth digging deep and accepting the truth of who you are and what you're capable of accomplishing? If you deny this power, your ego will win. You'll just be a crab in the bucket. Letting other people or circumstances create your reality is no way to live. As of today, you're no longer allowed to be a victim. You are finished with living small. Take a deep breath, my friend, and know you hold the power. You are a Remarkable Man!

THE EGO HAS LANDED

The insanity of the collective egoic mind, amplified by science and technology, is rapidly taking our species to the brink of disaster. Evolve or die: that is our only choice now.
— Eckhart Tolle

People say a little bit of ego is healthy, as long as it isn't too strong. Too strong? What does *that* mean? I've been in sales most of my life and have been around some big egos. We men are all about ego. Many men fail to understand that abrasiveness and bravado, along with confidence and assertiveness, are not as linked to the ego as one might think. Your ego does play a role in developing your character, but ego is too insidious to show its cards in the form of a character flaw or personality type.

The ego causes most of the world's challenges. To put it simply: Ego creates separation. Do not mistake your ego for a source of confidence and personal power, for it is not. Your ego controls you from the inside. Your subconscious mind constantly battles the duality your ego creates. Your ego wants things to remain as they are. It wants to prevent you from seeing the truth in your magnificence. Everyone has a baseline ego. It's where your comfort zone is established through experience and circumstance. Self-esteem and self-worth are established at an early age. These are the ego's baseline for establishing how much it can control you.

The real you is the empowered self, the student, and the teacher within. Your higher mind holds the truth of who you are. However, your ego isn't going to allow you to accept your truth without a fight. No matter how much you try, your ego will constantly bring you back to your baseline. Ego persistently tells you what a weak, fragile, insecure, and unworthy man you are—all lies.

My ego was as much in control of my life as was possible. You see, while my ego was set for insecurity, failure, and struggle, my higher self was set for success, abundance, and joy. However, I allowed my ego to run the show for the better part of my life. Ego endowed me with procrastination, laziness, and irresponsibility. Ego knew all my weaknesses and used them to destroy my dreams. My life of duality was set. I couldn't understand why everyone else seemed to be getting ahead and enjoying life. I did everything other people did to manifest my desires, yet my attraction capability was anything but what I desired...or so I thought.

Hindsight is always twenty-twenty. If I can save you a lifetime of frustration, confusion, and torment, I'm going to do it. I'm going to explain as clearly as I can, without any psychological, Freudian, clinical-speak, what and why you are where you are. Just like in the cartoons we watched as kids, where the devil and the angel perch themselves on the shoulders of a character who needs to make a difficult decision, your ego and your higher self place themselves similarly in your life. Instead of seeing religious icons, use an image of yourself. Replace the angel with your higher self, an image of you that's confident, happy, wise, and limitless. Replace the devil with your ego self, an image of you that's insecure, frustrated, angry, lonely, addicted, and selfish. Your competing selves don't just pop in once in awhile to guide your decision-making process. No, they're with you every moment of the day. Your head's in the middle, in a place of neutrality. Let's say the head is where "you" exist.

Your daily thoughts, all 60,000 or so of them, fall into one of three categories: neutral, ego-driven, or higher mind. If you want to know which thoughts control you, look at where you are in life. What shows up in your life, experiences, and circumstances is a result of who you put in charge at the gate. A Remarkable Man kicks the ego to the curb and takes control to end the dualistic struggle that keeps us from living dreams.

I want you to do yourself a favor and go to a place where there is a mirror. Look at yourself in the mirror and ask, out loud: "Who's in control of my life? Is it my ego or the real me?" As you look at yourself, you will see—with your own eyes—who's in charge. But you've always known. If your ego is in control, then you have some work to do, but it won't be as hard as you might think. If you're uncomfortable when you look at yourself, that's your ego doing its thing to widen the gap between your lower self and your higher self...the real you.

If you take the time to look deeply into yourself without the ego as the filter, you will see sadness, pain, and a host of other selves that the authentic self wants you to see. It will also allow you to see happiness, kindness, and other empowering aspects that exist within you too.

Most men don't understand the ego and how ego shows up in their lives. You'll be impressed when your perceptions open and you finally see "the truth" for what it is. Then your capacity for awareness opens, you grow, and a new and bigger truth comes in. You'll look back and realize your old truth was insignificant or just plain silly. When this happens, you're breaking free from your ego. Little by little, your true self builds a stronger case for who you truly are. Don't get me wrong here. Your ego *will* return with all its fury and history to pull you back, but it doesn't have the same impact it once did. Check one for the good guys! You just out-smarted your ego.

Over time, you'll have "Aha!" moments that allow you to understand more about how ego works in your life. Yes, you may go back into your ego often because as much as ego pulls you back or down, you have to admit that your comfort zone is well established. It can take a lifetime for some men to recognize and admit that they are operating from ego. Have you ever called someone on his ego, and he acquiesced and admitted it? Not likely, unless he had a considerable amount of self-awareness. You most likely got back an argument, a rebuttal, or a lashing.

A fish doesn't know it's in the water until the water's gone. Your higher self is attempting to pull you out of your ego so you can see ego for what it truly is: your lower self. Your lower self does not want you to grow. It's timid, weak, selfish, and frightened. Remember earlier when we talked about fear and its causes?

In order for me to show up in life, I knew I'd need to see my ego in a way that would make me so uncomfortable that I wouldn't want to be near it. What worked for me was to create an image of my ego that was loathsome, hideous, and so far removed from my true self that I pitied it. I imagined my ego perched on my left shoulder as a heroin addict, lost, weak, and alone. *How can this repulsive creature, my ego self, have any control over the person I'm becoming?* With this perspective, I finally saw the truth of who I was.

I also sent love to my ego. Yes, from your higher self, nothing is beneath you, and in order to cut your ego's control over your life, you must send it love. If you judge your ego, then you're no better than it is. When you love your ego from a heart-centered place, your ego-self will get what it's always wanted...acceptance, acknowledgment, and permission to leave.

Your lower selves reside within your ego. These selves, if ignored, will re-emerge to remind you of what you have not yet learned. Remember, you'll continue to get the lesson until you learn from it. Your higher self does not judge your lower selves. They are part of your growth. However, you'll release them faster if you admit you have them and acknowledge them for the lessons they provide.

Make a list of your lower selves. Be as honest as you can be. When you've made this list, you'll feel liberated because you've finally admitted these selves are present within you. With this list, they're out in the open. Do not judge yourself for having them, acknowledging them frees up space within you, and new, empowering selves will come in. List as many of the lower selves as you can, i.e., the greedy self, the unloving self, the hurtful self, the lonely self, and so on. Then take some time and go over each one thoroughly to discover what lesson each one has provided.

Acknowledge the lesson each lower self represents, and then go even deeper. Ask, "Have I truly learned the lesson?" Get real with yourself here. If you still hear from a certain lower self on a regular basis, chances are you're denying that it's there. You're doing everything you can do to avoid it. Since you can't run from yourself, that lower self will continue to poke, prod, and make your life miserable—and you'll wonder why you keep repeating certain experiences.

If you are willing to go to your truth, you will find that working on this list will bring up some powerful revelations and emotions. Perhaps there will be some pain in the truth. That's okay; allow yourself to feel it. This is *you* showing up for yourself! The movie of your life will change from a low-budget loser to an Oscar-winning theatrical success in a very short period.

Ego does not have to be the default setting for men. We are more than that. The Remarkable Man sees his magnificence and operates his life from this place of awareness.

If you've known all along that your ego has been in control, then this acknowledgment is probably difficult. You're probably focused on getting through this chapter! You're a man, and I get how you're wired. Your brain is trying to process all this information and put it in a context that will allow you to filter the information for your own needs and experiences.

I encourage you to continue to read and learn as much as you can from this book. However, I also want you to pause and reflect on what I've shared with you. I may have baked your noodle a little on understanding your ego and how it affects your life. So take a breather. Go on! I give you permission to bookmark this page and close the book right now to reflect and contemplate what you have learned.

Take a Break!

Welcome back. Now, let's return to shaking up your perceptions!

You must see ego as an aspect of yourself that you truly want to control. A few nights ago over dinner, I was talking with a friend about our dreams and desires. She said, "You know, I'm in a great position now and my ego wants to have it all; travel, a new luxury sports car, designer clothes, and the sense of freedom I've always wanted." Then she continued, "However, my higher self says I shouldn't be so greedy, ostentatious, or materialistic. Sometimes, I feel guilty for wanting my dreams. It seems too much for a spiritual person."

I responded with a challenge. I told her to reframe what she'd just said. "Your higher self says you *should* have it all," I explained. "You should travel, enjoy that new car, and have luxurious things in your life." It's true: your higher self says you can have everything you desire and still be your best spiritually. In reality, your ego self gives you those lower thoughts of guilt. Such thoughts put the brakes on your moving toward your desires.

The Universe wants the best for you. The Universe wants to give you everything you can imagine, without limitation. Your ego chimes in with ideas that are lower and undeserving, or it fills you with guilt. The ego loves to pull you down, to tell you to be "realistic," and to limit your imagination.

If you truly show up, you will realize you're acting out of ego any time you limit what you experience. When you're angry, judgmental, frustrated, anxious, controlling, weak—or any other limiting feeling, emotion, or action—you are in ego, plain and simple. The ego's number one agenda item is to keep you separated from your higher, true self. It battles to keep you in a duality meant to hold you back, and make the possible seem impossible.

My ego kept me in a state of limitation most of my life. My ego created circumstances that put me in fight or flight mode. Even with my awareness, my understanding of the Universe, and the personal growth I'd experienced, I still allowed ego to run my life. My higher self wasn't absent. On the contrary, it was patiently waiting to give me the power I needed when I needed it. The truth is I had a "better," more intimate relationship with my ego than I did with my higher self. Over the years, I'd allowed my lower feelings to become my default setting. Every time I tapped into my brilliance, my light would shine for a while. Universal energy, or your higher self, is stronger than your ego self, so your ego has little influence on new and empowering thoughts. For this reason, new ideas and empowering visions of yourself can continue for a while, unencumbered by limited thoughts. However, your ego knows that without constant action, a lack of momentum will eventually cause your ideas to slow down. The ego knows ideas need action, and that action only occurs in the physical world. It waits in ambush, and then it pounces. It reminds you that your resources are limited. It says people will judge you. It warns you that your goal will take long hours, and that "in truth," you're too lazy to pull off your dreams.

That was my life. It was really a crappy way to live. But I didn't know the truth. Okay, I knew it on some level, but I just wasn't ready to accept the fact that I was more powerful and responsible for my life than I could imagine. Wow! When I understood that, it hit home... and hard! In some way, it stung at first because when I reflected on my life with my newfound awareness, I regretted the excitement and opportunities I'd missed. It saddened me to realize how much more vibrant my life would have been if I'd known where I was operating from and how much my ego was in control.

Something that was always hard for me to accept was that many things are time-coded for your specific journey; they match your maturity and ability to handle them. Lessons come and repeat themselves to match your growth. I interpreted this timing as meaning that I was living by fate, and if I allowed myself to live with that idea, then I wasn't in control of my life. It meant something outside of me was pulling the strings. Why bother if puppet-strings and the stars are in control? However, thankfully, I learned I could have power over "fate." If anything were time-coded, this lesson was one of them.

Yes, you have power over fate. When you operate from ego, you aren't in control of your life. You're leaving it up to others. This lack of control is the ego world. Your higher self wants you to be in control. You do that by taking charge with your energy, knowledge, love, passion, and power.

Freedom is yours to claim. "You" can show up in an instant if that's what you want. It is only as difficult as you perceive it to be. I'm not trying to make light of your current situation, especially if you are in a place in life where everything is showing up as struggle and limitation. How does it feel to know you're living from your ego self? Ouch! It stings, doesn't it? Are you feeling some resistance to that idea? Maybe there's a knot or uneasy feeling in your stomach. Yes, your feeling center knows the truth and reveals all.

Men, you are NOT your ego! You've just been sold a bill of goods meant to keep you from your truth. Being in your ego, and thus experiencing so many limitations, is not a condemnation of who you are. Remember, I lived from that place most of my life. It sucks, big-time! Take stock of the feelings your ego can create. All of them! Here is a partial list:

- Fear

- Anger

- Frustration

- Guilt

- Worry

- Separation

- Worthlessness

- Weakness

- Hatefulness

- Jealousy

- Spite

- Victimization

- Deception

- Untruthfulness

- Envy

- Abandonment

- Powerlessness

- Limitedness

- Sadness

- Loneliness

- Being Closed-off

- Resentfulness

When you operate from these feelings, your ego is in control. Ouch!

Yes, the truth can be hard at times, but liberating too. Look over the list, study it, and know it. Add any ego-created feelings you have. If you get this idea, and truly want to understand yourself and why you function the way you do, you will understand the devious relationship ego has with you.

When I first looked at this list, it was both maddening and humbling. Maddening because I refused to believe I was in my ego that much. I embodied a great deal of that list and rejected the concept that it was all because of me being in my ego. But then, I didn't fully understand the ego's nature. I'd thought it meant I was full of myself, a blowhard, a jerk! But when I understood the true meaning, the list humbled me because it revealed a truth: I wasn't a happy person. That list represented more of my life than I wanted to admit.

It also revealed how I probably appeared to those who were close to me. Yes, the mirror was unkind to me. I saw a man who was beaten and used up, a man who'd let his light grow dim. When I looked at my reflection, I asked myself and God, "How am I supposed to live from this place? My God, this isn't fun!" When you get real with yourself in front of the mirror, emotions tend to come to the surface easier. Not only that, but the separated self and the victim self have a good shot at being heard. Admit it! You've had a meltdown or two in front of the mirror. Yes, we men hold in our emotions and feelings a lot. However, I'm sure every one of you has gravitated to the mirror for an emotional purge at some point. You know you've cried out, "Why me? I'm a good person! Please, please! Help me!" or any number of pleas and self-deprecating statements such as, "How could I have been so stupid?" or "I'm a loser," and so on. The mirror also shows you your truth because you go to it to come to terms with your ego. Once the purging is over, the cleansing begins.

The emotional release moves away your ego's lower emotions and makes way for your higher self to come through. A shift occurs and you start to feel the answers. Sometimes, you may laugh at your state of mind. As your power strengthens, between each sniffle and blowing of the nose, a smirk or a laugh blurts out as you realize the silliness of it all. Within a few minutes, the strength inside you starts to take over. A feeling of muted euphoria begins to rise as you understand who you are. Then you feel a sensation of connection, love, and power that is quite beautiful. Your tears of pain soon become tears of hope, understanding, and freedom.

Your ego wants you to feel closed-off and separate from your dreams. The longer you hold that energy, the more your ego gains strength to keep you in a limited world. Not only that, but due to the nature of the energetic vibration of the lower world, you can manifest much more than lower feelings. Your health and wellbeing can suffer too. Ego wants to keep you under its control and has a plethora of propaganda, misinformation, and manipulation at its disposal. Your health is yours and yours alone. If you're feeling your lower energies, depending on their severity, you have many options to deal with them. Ego, however, wants to limit those options. Ego is reactive in its approach to your health. The higher self is proactive and focuses on prevention.

What baffles me most about the ego and its connection to health is the utter blindness ego can have about life-and-death choices. I'm referring to the mainstream medical and pharmaceutical community, industries based on pure ego. It saddens me to hear about people in a downward spiral who put all their hopes in a drug to make them feel better. Worse are the drugs featured in two-minute commercials where more than half of the commercial is the disclaimer listing all the side effects the drug could have. The side effects are hideous, absurd, and shocking, yet companies are allowed to market drugs to an uneducated and overmedicated population. This cycle is ego feeding ego!

As a Remarkable Man, you must take full responsibility for your health. Want to see how much control the ego has over you? Check your medicine cabinet. How many prescription drugs do you see? If you take prescription medications, be honest with yourself. Are the drugs working? Or are you justifying your use of them to mask a bigger problem?

I know there are many "wonder drugs" out there that have done amazing things for humanity and have saved the lives of millions. However, I am referring to those drugs that are prone to adverse side effects and addiction. The sad truth is that your prescription drugs are rarely there to cure you of the disease (*Dis*-ease) you are experiencing. Just like the ego, drugs only mask the problem. We live in a quick-fix, make-me-better, it's-out-of-my control-world.

I am not a medical expert and in no way can advise on your unique situation. However, I am grateful to have had my eyes opened years ago when it comes to the truth about the drug industry. When I spiraled into depression, I chose not to take drugs to help me feel better. I've seen the effects antidepressant medications can have on people. They don't get the quick fix they expect. Plus, many people don't take into account the long-term effects of these drugs. I was blessed because my higher self had enough power over my ego to seek help through coaching (my sister, Karen, was amazing) and go within rather than looking to the outside for help. If you choose meds as your solution, just make sure you have all the answers and that you need to make the most informed decision. It is your health and your life we are talking about here.

I go into health in much more detail in the next chapter, but please understand just how controlling the ego can be when it comes to your health. Remember, your ego wants to separate you from who you really are. If you are seeking to cover up, mask, and medicate your health challenges, then your ego may be running the show. If you are seeking health, vitality, and nutrition through an active lifestyle, education, and awareness, then your higher self is leading the charge.

Let's shift gears away from your ego and examine what you can do to get your ego under control. If you want to change your circumstances, you'll have to shift gears in the moment. Just writing that sentence prompted memories of my journey toward becoming Remarkable. Okay, I need to share another truth with you. You must know by now that I was reluctant to let go of my ego. There's knowing what needs to be done in order to change, and then there's having the will or desire to change. Even in my victim or lack cycles, I fought to continue the experience. Crazy, right? Recognizing I was in ego was both challenging and frustrating. Even though I knew my stance or argument was solely coming from ego, I couldn't release it. This recognition may be the hardest part about being a Remarkable Man. You have the awareness to set a new direction, and you must trust your higher self to take over and guide you to where you want to go.

Just like the ego, the higher self comes with a complete set of emotions and feelings. For the most part, these feelings are opposite in energy from those of your ego. When you recognize these feelings, you'll know you have shifted and are in tune with your higher self.

You may experience feelings of:

- Confidence
- Purpose
- Love
- Excitement
- Passion
- Kindness
- Understanding
- Compassion
- Freedom
- Power

- Success

- Connection

- Knowing

- Truth

- Honor

- Valor

- Integrity

- Trust

- Openness

- Harmony

- Focus

- Awareness

- Oneness

- Respect

- Courage

- Hope

- Peace

- Joy

I am sure you can think of a few more that work for you. The point is that in order to have these feelings and emotions, you must be connected to your higher self. Ego takes a vacation in these moments. Study this list, and become familiar with the moments and situations you associate with each one of these feelings. Then lock in the understanding that when you have these feelings, those are the times when you have control. That is when you have the power to be Remarkable! When you reach that state, you have the power to do, be, and have the life you want.

It all comes from the higher self, your truth. Use this understanding to make the adjustments you need to bring the "fate" you desire into your life. Everything is energy, and now, you can begin to attract the experiences you want in life.

Ego has nothing to do with confidence, authenticity, and self-control. Ego is present when you are in the "Look at me, I'm better than you" world. Most men don't think they're in ego when they're low, disconnected, and helpless. Any feelings that keep you separate, angry, or unhappy are the work of your ego. Your higher self is patient, understanding, and compassionate. It's waiting for you to show up and find your power over ego. Your higher self is waiting for you to accept the truth of who you are. Be kind to yourself as you move through the process.

Are you ready to sever the ties between you and your ego? *The Remarkable Man* book and the Remarkable Man Project are here to help you shed your ego-centered image. You're better than that. You're ready to break the pattern and spell of your ego's control. The Remarkable Man removes the *ego* masculine and embraces the *authentic* masculine.

ESSENTIAL #5

REMARKABLE ACTION

You who have dreams; if you act, they will come true.
To turn your dream to a fact, it's up to you.
— From *Stout-Hearted Men*, by Sigmund Romberg/Oscar Hammerstein II

Most everyone has heard of the "Bucket List." You know, a list of things you want to achieve or experience before you die. Before that concept came along, it was called a wish list, a dream list, or what have you. Whatever term you choose, the list is something to inspire you to reach higher and go farther than you have before. Completing this list says, "I've lived!" I bet you've created at least two such lists in your lifetime. Here's the thing: When most people do this exercise, they do it from a place of fantasy. "Yeah, it sure would be nice to sky dive, or learn to fly." So they make a list, knowing they really have no intention—at their core—that they'll really do it. Well, buckle up! The Remarkable Man Project includes creating a "Champion's List" and setting the gauge to "Done!" I want you to visualize every item as done—not wishful thinking, not a joke to fill up another line on the sheet, but an actual accomplishment.

Let's get to it! Take out a piece of paper or write on a page in your journal. Write at the top in bold letters: **My Champion's List.** Now just list everything you can imagine a Remarkable Man like yourself should experience. Write until the page is full. This will tell you what your higher self needs to experience...because this is what came first.

I know many of you have done this exercise before, but bear with me. As I've said, some things are time-coded and you get the message on a different or deeper level than you did before. The message here is of a Remarkable one.

Now that you have your Champion's List complete, I want you to go back and circle the ten items that are your most important "Must-Haves." Just ten! The reason is that out of all the items you have listed, most will end up as wallpaper. There probably isn't enough traction in your life to complete every one of them. Look, I'm just being honest with you. Yes, some of you could prove me wrong and hit every one of your dreams out of the park! If so, good on ya! I want that for all of you. But if you narrow it down to just ten remarkable experiences, your odds of getting them done will increase.

Now, with the top ten circled on your Champion's List, I want you to picture each one as done. Visualize each one for about thirty seconds. You can spend longer time with this later. For now, what you're doing is planting a seed of possibility for your subconscious to comprehend. Nothing is impossible to a Remarkable Man. What's cool is that The Remarkable Man Project is going to help you get them done.

That's right! The Remarkable Man Project is an international membership of Remarkable Men doing Remarkable things that inspire, uplift, and move you to be, do, and have more. Also, you'll have a positive impact on the people who matter most in your life. The Champion's List is a way you can connect with other Remarkable Men and achieve your dreams. Action is at the core of the Remarkable Man. You must become a man who is a doer, not just a talker. The trick is to turn doing what must be done from drudgery to having a lot of fun along the way.

Taking action for what you know you want to do comes with curses and rewards. In order to make it happen, physical action will be involved. No amount of dreaming, praying, or affirmations will make the law of attraction work for you unless you include physical action. Taking action sets a cause in motion. You'll go from knowing what needs to happen to taking action to watch your business and personal relationships flourish. If you're single, what actions do you need to take to meet the girl of your dreams? How does a Remarkable Man interact with the people in his life? When a man takes action for what's important in his life, he becomes an unstoppable force, and that speaks volumes about who he is.

When in your life have you procrastinated about taking action? As men, we know what we must do, but for some reason, taking action to make it happen gets the same response as the items on our "Bucket Lists." Come on; admit it! You know you need to accomplish some huge action items in order to get from where you are to where you want to be.

There is power within the law of attraction that very few people understand. Let me explain. Imagine you're the director of an amazing movie, a blockbuster. This movie is titled, *My Life*. It's a simple title, with a clear and obvious plot. You control the actors, scenes, and script for this movie. With this responsibility, are you going to create an award-winning movie, or will it be another low-budget flop? It's your call.

Get clear on the movie of your life as it is now. Are the set, cast, and crew to your liking? In your eyes, is the plot powerful enough to create a box-office smash? Do you have the support you need to see it through to completion? If not, do not despair. The Universe wants to help you. The energy to create your life, your life movie, is all around you. Right here, right now. However, the Universe is timeless. It is not bound by linear progress, so it will wait patiently for your true self to show up when you are ready. The challenge is that you have a finite number of days in this lifetime to experience all you desire. So it is incumbent upon you to live each day in pursuit of creating a life movie worth sharing. I also want you to imagine that as you are filming the *My Life* movie, a documentary crew follows you around to keep you honest and catch your every emotion and deed.

You know you must take full responsibility for your life. Also, you know you must master your ego. Now, let's start with being responsible for your movie studio's set-up. Is it big enough? Do you need to stretch your imagination? Are you being conservative with your production because you feel you've been too grandiose in the past? Stop the tape now! If this is the case, you cannot put more film in the main camera to shoot or you'll be disappointed once again. Remember, the documentary people are following you around to remind you of how well your production is going. Self-responsibility tells you that you must be clear with what you want for your life. Who do you need to play the supporting roles? Who do you want to audition? Financially, how much backing do you need to make it happen?

Once you get clear on these details and have your storyboard laid out the way you envision it, the Universe will go into action to bring it all together. Your conviction and determination to change your life will help the Universe help you. This energy cannot come to you until you project it out!

Have you ever wondered why it sometimes takes so long to manifest what you want? Have you thought you've done everything you can do, only to have nothing come of it? How many times have you felt as though everything is in alignment and the magic seems to happen? Why do these seemingly disconnected moments occur? Is it random luck or something more? Let me give you an image of how synchronicity works and why things happen the way they do.

Have some fun with me for a moment. Imagine that the Universe, God, Energy, angels, guides, teachers, or ascended masters—whatever you choose to call your higher power—assembled in a large control room. Picture a room such as NASA's Mission Control. Specialists, engineers, and scientists are moving about, keeping a watchful eye on giant screens, or huddled in front of hundreds of computer monitors. Instead of NASA personnel, *this* room employs the angels, guides, and energy of the Universe. They are sitting in their chairs monitoring many screens. However, instead of seeing information or data, they see "interference" similar to the static you sometimes see on the old TVs when a channel had no signal. Although it might look like nothing is happening on the screens, those who've been assigned to watch them are focused and engaged. The reason they watch so attentively is that every little white dot in the chaos represents a point of light. Each light is an individual soul here on Earth. And look! On one monitor, down near the front and to the right, is where—that's right!—your light is flickering too!

There you are, going about your business, unaware of the light you are emitting. The program running behind the scenes does something unique as well. It measures the intensity of light coming from each person. So, as your guides watch you, they see you're creating the movie of your life. Then suddenly, you are inspired, some creative genius takes hold, and you feel a sense of purpose and passion for what you want. While your passion for this new idea takes hold, your light begins to grow as you take authentic action! You continue and put forth more energy and action toward your dream. Your light's intensity keeps growing, until it triggers an alarm on the screen. Your light has grown brighter and shines more powerfully than the millions of dots around you. You begin to stand out on the screen! One of the angels assigned to that monitor takes note of your now-flashing light and taps a few keys to zoom in on your bright little beacon. Then, a file pops up with all the details of who you are.

"Well now, what do we have here?" the guide asks curiously. It watches you with excited anticipation that you are serious about the life you are creating. It observes your thoughts, energy, and actions for a while (this could be days or weeks, since the Universe is not time-bound). Then, after assessing your project, it is convinced that you have something worthy of assistance from the Universe. The guide leans over to a colleague who's concentrating on a bright light on another screen. "Hey, check this out. Look at what my file is up to." Remember, that "file" is you!

The guide gestures to the point on the screen where you are happily putting forth effort and action to pull together your life plan. Then the guide enthusiastically says, "This file has the right stuff! I like the plan and the energy. It just feels right. What do you think?"

The colleague-guide squints and massages its chin. "Yeah, I think you've got something there. I like it!" The other guide adds, "You know, I have someone on my screen who would be perfect for a supporting role in that vision."

"Really?" says the first one as it looks over to the other screen.

"Take a look. They seem to match up well."

"Okay, let's put them together. How about we put them in the same networking event and let them do their thing?"

Then a supervisor strolls by and inquires, "What's going on here?"

The two guides are excited and respond at once with tangled-up exuberance.

The supervisor put up its hand to stop them. "Slow down. One at a time!"

The guide at the monitor where your light is flashing takes a deep gulp and explains, "I have a person here who has a great idea and is pushing hard to make it a reality." Then the guide motions to its colleague's monitor and continues, "Over here, we have someone with a big vision too. It looks like he could be a great match in moving things forward!"

The supervisor, wise with experience, shakes its head and says, "I see they are both of equal brilliance. And yes, they could be a great match, but let's hold on a few minutes and see what happens."

Remember, "a few minutes" in the Universe's control room is more of a slang term since time is irrelevant.

As they patiently watch the screens, something begins to happen. Down on Earth, you are working hard on your plan, but then the phone rings. One of your friends wants to go out for a night on the town. You say you can't go because you're working on your project and don't have time.

Your friend asks, "What's this *project*?" You hear the sanctimonious tone in his voice.

You hesitate because you're not ready to let the cat out of the bag. You wanted to be a little further along before you told your not-very-supportive, but well-meaning friend. You hesitate, but then you tell him. But your energy isn't where it needs to be, so you sound a little soft and cautious.

Your friend responds with, "Really? You're going to be an entrepreneur? Your last dream didn't pan out well, you know. What makes you think it's going to happen this time?" On and on he goes, and at the end of his rant, he says, "C'mon! Don't be a stick in the mud; come out to play."

Bam! Your bright light has taken its first hit—and you begin to doubt yourself. You don't realize there's a crab in your bucket. You begin to think about the mistakes you made in the past...and your light grows dimmer. You start to make choices that are not in keeping with your dreams...your light grows weaker still. Before you know it...your light has faded away.

"See, there you have it," the supervisor says knowingly. "You can't assume these bright lights are genuine. You have to give them time to find out who they really are." As the supervisor moves on to the next work station, the two hopeful angels swivel their chairs back around and let out a collective sigh of disappointment. Still, they understand that being your cheerleader requires patience.

A few days pass and you can't stand the rut you're in. You've gone out with your friend for another empty evening of the same old thing. You deserve much more and you know it. You see your business plan peeking out from under a stack of drawings and clippings of your vision. You realize that you only feel alive when you're following your passion. But is it really in you? Can you make it happen this time?

You take a triumphant, deep breath and proclaim your commitment. "I'm going to make this happen," you say to the Universe. "And I don't care what anyone says or thinks!" Suddenly, you're awash with a "can-do" sense of power and purpose. You find yourself working, learning, and planning to get your vision rolling. It's well after midnight, and most other nights, you'd put on the brakes to go to sleep. But you aren't tired; there's a fire burning within, and you feel your strength and sense of self grow stronger. You don't respond to phone calls or people who are "crabs in your bucket." You make good choices and know you are on your path. A Remarkable Man is emerging... and you can feel it!

Back at the Universe's control center, our two dutiful angels are pulling a late shift when, suddenly, your light pops up on the screen! The angel checks out the file. It's you...It's YOU! With excitement, the angel shouts, "My friend is back." Then, pointing to the computer screen, "Check it out!"

The other angel swivels around with a cautious smile. "Remember what the supervisor said," it whispers cautiously.

"I know, I know, but this time it's different...look at these readings! They're off the charts!"

So they wait and watch...like excited football fans watching their favorite team in the Super Bowl on TV in their living room. They truly want the best for you and cheer you on.

You're determined; you aren't worried about the "how-to's" now. You're focused on the big vision. You're making calls, setting up meetings by day, planning and perfecting your vision at night.

Suddenly, the white flashing light that is you changes intensity. It is now a brilliant ball of golden light! "Wow! My friend is making it happen," the angel shouts.

The supervisor strolls by with its hands behind its back. In a soft, sage tone it says, "I've been watching this one, too, with some interest. I think it's time." The supervisor puts his hand firmly on the angels' shoulders. "Let's make it happen."

The two angels, giddy with joy, turn to their keyboards and begin tapping away codes and sequences. "Synchronicity Sequence ALPHA now!" And with one final click of the mouse, "Engaged!" The two angels high-five each other, and with colossal grins, they settle in to watch what unfolds.

So, there you are with your wonderful vision and passion for life. You feel it at your core. A supportive friend calls and suggests the two of you get together for coffee. You arrive at the appointed time, but just as you pay for your coffee and newspaper, your friend calls to say that there's been a last-minute emergency and he won't be able to make it. You find yourself perplexed, maybe a little put out, but then decide you might as well sit back and enjoy your coffee.

You take a seat and scan the room without noticing anyone in particular. The man at the table next to you seems to be waiting for someone. You pay little attention and even avoid eye contact for a while as you get settled in. You take out your PDA and pretend to busy yourself with it. That gets old, and the newspaper doesn't hold your interest, either. You sigh as you look around the coffee shop. A young interior designer is showing color swatches to her client. Two well-dressed businessmen are sharing a laptop screen and talking about numbers. Three school girls are animated and chatty. You see what appears to be an online blind date between an athletic young man and a woman with a few extra pounds who likely put "shapely" in her profile. You perceive the date isn't going well. Finally, your scan of the coffee shop returns to the man at the table beside you. A barista appears with free samples of a seasonal treat. She stands between the two of you with the tray of delights, so you each take a sample. Voila! Instant icebreaker! You both nod and comment on the tasty surprise. With his mouth half full, your "neighbor" says, "I love it when they do this. It tells me I'm in the right place at the right time."

Well, *you* love it when you hear that kind of language. "I hear you," you respond. "That was a good one!" Then, sensing there's more to this meeting than pure chance, you continue, "I noticed you seem to be waiting for someone. Are they running late?"

With a sigh, he replies, "Yes. I mean no. She had to cancel. We were going to talk about finding a new project to invest in."

You smile and can't believe the synchronicity. You get the sense that everything is perfect, and inside, you give the Universe a "Thank you."

Now, your experience is unique to you. The point is you've had seemingly chance encounters all your life, and they've played both big and small roles to move you forward. The Universe always works with you to bring you more of what you're vibrating about. You owe it to yourself to be vigilant of your thoughts. They pack a punch and determine how brightly your light will shine.

Back at the Universe's control center, the angels are busy putting all the bright lights together in direct relation to their brilliance. The ups and downs you experience in life, and the people you manifest, are all products of your will.

Thinking of your life as a movie and imagining the Universal control center are methods to help you understand the deeper aspects of your power. This practice is also a great way to understand how much control you have over your life. In order to be a Remarkable Man, you must remain in control of the movie of your life. No one but you has the right to write your script, build your set, or develop the plot. This movie is your domain, and you must own this truth if your life is to move in the direction you desire.

Keep shining your light and know that the Universe notices everything. Keep believing in your dreams and do not despair if things are not happening as quickly as you think they should. Everything will unfold as soon as you're capable of handling it.

SELF-DISCIPLINE

The best day of your life is the one on which you decide your life is your own. No apologies or excuses. No one to lean on, rely on, or blame. The gift is yours—it is an amazing journey—and you alone are responsible for the quality of it. This is the day your life really begins.
— Bob Moawad

The level of self-discipline in your life is a reflection of the global self-image you have for yourself. Without doubt, self-discipline is part of the process of becoming a Remarkable Man, especially after we've talked about taking action.

I have a confession to make, and it is a very telling one at that. The struggles and challenges throughout my life were indeed a product of the duality my ego wanted to create. I created stories for each chapter of my life to serve the predicaments I found myself in. These stories, however, were not always the truth. They were *my* truth, but they served more as convenient coping mechanisms to absolve me of any blame or responsibility. I often lamented and railed at the Universe. After all, I had the gifts and talents to make it big and succeed at anything I put my energy toward. Yet somehow, I never quite caught the proverbial Golden Goose.

Knowing and understanding how something works is just education. It's brain food, but it won't get you very far. To have true wisdom, you must put your knowledge into action. I know I am preaching to the converted here, and this is not a new revelation, but stay with me here.

I had a habit of starting new projects, areas of learning, or business ideas. I would learn all I could for a while and then coast, thinking the product would be a sure-fire success. Of course, I'd fall flat on my face, pissed off at the world for my failure. I was what you'd call a dabbler, someone who started, gave a little effort, and then wondered why success didn't follow.

Talent without discipline is like an octopus on roller skates.
There's plenty of movement, but you never know if it's going to be
forward, backwards, or sideways.
— H. Jackson Brown, Jr.

Earlier, I wrote about time and explained why it's critical to manage time well. I also shared a key component to effective time management that I lacked: self-discipline. In my delusional worldview, a little effort gave me the luxury to float for a while. This went against all my self-development education, which said, "Get busy!" For this reason, I had boom and bust cycles in my life. I did not have the self-discipline I needed to maintain the constant effort necessary to attain and sustain my goals, dreams, and desires.

The cool thing I came to realize, far beyond everything I'd learned over the years, was that I didn't have to invent a plan, tactic, or tool to get where I wanted to go. The direction and path had been laid for me by those who'd succeeded in the same pursuits. Still, there are no shortcuts to success. You can choose ease and grace on the journey, but you still need to put in the effort. Say, for example, you want to get into the best shape of your life. You can choose from two paths. There's the purely physical appearance of being physically fit, and there's the whole mind-body concept of being in shape. If physical appearance is your goal, some would suggest cosmetic surgery as a shortcut to avoid self-discipline and effort. Well, yes, but you know you'd be cheating yourself too, and you wouldn't be in the best shape of your life, through and through.

Smart self-discipline occurs when you realize other people have been exactly where you are. Then you can look at what they did to get them where *you* want to be. Your self-discipline now turns to making the goal as real and as motivating as you can imagine. What will your life be like when you are in the best shape of your life? What kind of social life will you have? What kind of people will you hang out with? What might you accomplish with your newfound confidence? What will your new wardrobe look like? Whatever you use to make your outcome more compelling is part of the self-discipline required to get you started, build momentum, and complete your goal.

Now, this is the simple part of the task. This is still the "mind" component. To get in the best shape of your life, you'll need a great deal of the "physical" component. So instead of deciding to go it alone and rely on an already shaking level of self-discipline, seek help. Model your routine after those who have gone before you. Better yet, team up with a friend or colleague to challenge, motivate, and empower each other toward your goals. Go a step further and hire a fitness trainer or coach to guide you to your dream. Be sure to tell your coach or partner where you are weak in your self-discipline. Tell as many people as you can, and ask them to help you be accountable to yourself and your goals. If you have a problem getting up early, tell someone. If you have a hard time sticking with your diet, tell someone. If a weakness has previously blocked your progress, this area is where your partner or coach can help you stay on course.

You can make the process as easy or as difficult as you want it to be, but know that for every goal, there's a way to make it real. If you're going to get in the best shape of your life, you'll need a level of commitment you may have never experienced. It may require being at the gym at five o'clock in the morning, running in the rain, and pushing through mental barriers. It may require reeducating yourself about food and supplements, eating routines, food preparation, and letting go of foods you love that are not conducive to being in the "best shape of your life."

Getting into the best shape of your life can be very simple. You just have to be disciplined enough to follow a set of steps that have proven to get the results you want. Will it be easy? Probably not, but it will be what you want it to be. I know people who have rewired themselves and become 100 percent dedicated to their health and fitness. They look amazing and have such energy and enthusiasm. Yet the year before, they were lethargic, overweight, and unhappy.

Everything, and I mean everything, you want to achieve is laid out before you. The methods and techniques are varied and diverse. Reading about it and watching videos about it can educate you, but you need to put the education into action and make it happen.

You know in your heart that you cannot become a Remarkable Man without self-discipline. We all have behavioral patterns that either move us forward or slow us down. Being a Remarkable Man will require you to become cognizant of the activity you're involved in on a moment by moment basis. This awareness will challenge your purpose and passion more than you can imagine, but it will do more for your sense of self than anything you've ever tried.

You see, every activity we engage in either moves us toward or away from our goals. When we operate with this realization, we find more clarity, direction, and results. Using the "best shape of your life" example, if you hit the snooze alarm because it's too dark or rainy instead of going for a run or heading to the gym, does that move you toward or away from your goal?

If you have an extra slice of pizza on your "cheat" day, will that move you toward or away from your goal? If you watch a reality show instead of reading about health and wellness, does that move you toward or away from your goal? You can see where I'm going with this.

Systems, systems, systems! Implementing systems was one of the best tools I discovered to finish this book. I realized I needed to create a system and plan to make it happen. I studied my heroes and mentors who've written books to learn about their writing habits and techniques. However, my biggest motivator was the simple fact that my book would never be a reality unless I started.

I admired the discipline and dedication of the authors I studied. They paved the way for me to write this book. From this place, I knew it was possible for me too. They were not any better than me; they just had the will and the discipline to push through their own mental barriers to realize a dream. If they could do it, then I could do it too.

I had to come to terms with my daily routine. What was moving me toward the completion of my book? What was moving me away from it? What thoughts built my image of myself as a great writer, and what thoughts pulled me down? This way of thinking and self-discipline began to transcend all other aspects of my life because I began to clean up a lot of unwanted baggage in my life, including people, activities, and focus. I became a powerhouse of focusing on what I truly desired. The Universe saw my light growing and shining brightly. I experienced synchronicity and opportunity almost daily. Finally, the magic I'd witnessed in other people's lives was happening in mine. Flow that was once illusive and often invisible was now abundantly clear and obvious.

I want you to think, and be as honest as you can, about what you need to do in order to start being a Remarkable Man. You know you are responsible for your experiences and the people you have manifested in your life. You know there's a direct path to help you achieve anything you want in life. So here's the $64,000 question: How much do you want it? What compelling desire will charge you up to take authentic, inspired action toward your goal? Self-discipline will be born out of your compelling desire.

Self-discipline transcends your small self and unifies you with all that is. Self-discipline aligns you with your commitment to your journey. The benefits of self-discipline are more profound than you might imagine. An obvious benefit is that you'll achieve more in less time. You'll have more control of your day. Additionally, you'll notice that others treat and respond to you differently than before. I can guarantee there are some people in your life who have a strong level of self-discipline. You know what self-discipline has allowed those friends to accomplish, and you know how you feel about them. When we think about our friends who have self-discipline, we have feelings of respect, admiration, and appreciation.

As you leave this chapter, I want you to take it to heart and think about where you stand when it comes to the level of self-discipline in your life. Make this chapter work for you by creating a list of areas where you feel you're weak. And I mean all of them. For some, self-discipline is a serious challenge and can even be life-threatening. Do you drink too much? Do you do drugs? Are you prone to emotional or physical violence? If it's a serious problem, then seek help—fast. If you are borderline in these, or any other, dangerous behaviors, I hope your desire to become a Remarkable Man will give you the self-discipline you need to keep from taking that extra drink, doing more drugs, or hurting the people you care about.

Please take this exercise seriously. Then ask yourself, "What stories am I telling myself and others about why I can or cannot do anything I want?" How many times do you have to tell yourself, "Today is the day I become the person I know I am," only to fall back to your old patterns just a few days later?

Becoming a Remarkable Man is about letting go of the story that you are a quitter, a loser, or a non-completer. Today you are you! No labels, excuses, or "Yeah, buts!" You are a person with incredible potential and power. Even more, you're ready to move from where you are to where you desire to be. Start showing up today by finding a direct path toward whatever goal you seek. Start today to read, study, and model those who have done it before you. Set up a system of accountability. Plan your day completely, from morning to night, to stay on track and hold yourself to a higher standard. Remember to be kind to yourself and allow for "Me" time and family time.

It may be necessary to take an aggressive stance with your life if self-discipline has been an issue in the past. Get a grasp on those bright, shiny objects that distract and throw you off course. Finish one task at a time, and reward yourself for doing so. Over time, you will shed the story that you are easily distracted. Being Remarkable will begin to be the norm for you. Let go of the story that it's hard for you to focus. Instead, just see it as a series of simple steps that, with the assistance of self-discipline, will help you achieve all you can imagine.

Self-discipline is a form of freedom. Freedom from laziness and lethargy, freedom from the expectations and demands of others, freedom from weakness and fear—and doubt.
— H.A. Dorfman

COURAGE TO BE MEN

Come to the edge, He said.
They said: We are afraid.
Come to the edge, He said.
They came. He pushed them,
And they flew.
— Guillaume Apollinaire

I remember hearing one of my all-time favorite inspirational heroes, Les Brown, talk about being bold. He said, "...if you are not completing or following your passion and purpose, it is akin to committing spiritual suicide." I took his words to heart. They're words worth living by.

Being a Remarkable Man means standing up for your beliefs. When you fail to follow through on your plans and passions, a part of you dies. You have probably felt this loss many times in your life, so you know what I am saying is true. You feel it when you stay in bed, even though the night before, you were committed and determined to get up early and go to the gym. The regret and disappointment behind your excuses haunts you the rest of the day. And you know how hard it becomes to live with yourself if you continue to procrastinate on your dreams. Having a Remarkable life will require the courage necessary to break the barriers that have held you back.

You are reading this book at the perfect time and at the perfect place in your life. This experience is not an accident. Your light is shining brightly and aches for you to manifest the shifts and changes that are seemingly bursting inside you. Trust this feeling as the calling within that will challenge and spur you on to take steps toward what you were born to do. The courage you require is within, and you know it. This time, it's different. You realize that being Remarkable is not so far away from where you are now. Finding courage, strength, and power will no longer require a huge effort as it did in the past. None-theless, it is imperative that you begin at once to play the game in a new way. Take little steps of courage every day to push the envelope from the person you are now to the person you're becoming. With-out a doubt, making it a goal to stretch your comfort level at least once each day opens up a world of opportunity and experiences.

There is magic in being courageous. Everyone wants to do it, but few actually experience it daily. Your courage puts you at an admirable advantage. Know this fact and you may see how to add courage to your day. Courage does not have to entail great feats of bravery, risk-ing your life, or proving anything to anyone. Courage is having faith and trust in yourself and using your talents to their fullest. Once I grasped the global aspect of courage, I understood it on a deeper level. When you realize that the playing field of life is level, you will see how easy it is to add courage to your life.

Most men have a similar list of challenges and insecurities. Yes, even the men you hold in high esteem. The men who seem to have it all together and ooze self-confidence share these feelings. These feelings are the great leveler of us all. Be honest and ask yourself how many of these traits you have.[1]

1. You have a tendency to be critical of yourself.

2. You have a great need for people to like and admire you.

1 Taken from: Forer, B. R. (1949) "The Fallacy of Personal Validation: A Classroom Demonstration of Gullibility," Journal of Abnormal Psychology, 44: 118-121

3. You have a great deal of unused capacity and have not used it to your advantage.

4. While you have some personality weaknesses, you are generally able to compensate for them.

5. Disciplined and self-controlled outside, you tend to be worrisome and insecure inside.

6. At times (and recently more often), you have doubts as to whether you have made the right decision or done the right thing.

7. You prefer a certain amount of change and variety, and become dissatisfied when hemmed in by restrictions and limitations.

8. You pride yourself on being an independent thinker, and don't accept others' statements without satisfactory proof.

9. You have found it unwise to be too frank in revealing yourself to others.

10. Some of your aspirations tend to be unrealistic.

11. Security is one of your major goals in life, even though you sometimes wish it weren't.

How many did you check? If you were being truly honest with yourself, you most likely checked all of them. This list by Dr. Forer illuminates a truth. Every person—at one level or another—has these same doubts and insecurities. I checked every one when I first went through the list. No matter how much we profess to be masters of our minds and circumstances, part of us hangs onto our ego's need for acceptance and recognition.

I share this list with you because once you get beyond your own limitations and understand that you are not alone, you'll realize the whole world wants and needs to feel something more. Then you can be the one who gives it to them. That's right! This is where a little bit of courage gives you an immediate advantage over everyone else.

In other words, once you understand how desperate humanity is to be encouraged, assured, and uplifted, then the courage you need can be as simple as giving a sincere compliment or a smile with assuring eye contact. A businessman in an expensive suit may appear to have power, abundance, and confidence, but he is putty in your hands if you compliment the cut and style of his suit.

A woman who puts effort into her hair, make-up, shoes, and accessories longs to hear validation for her fashion choices. I am not talking about vanity and insecurity. I am talking about a basic truth. A compliment costs us nothing, but the benefits continue. Frankly, adding courage, enthusiasm, sincerity, and compliments to your daily activities will change your life.

When I order coffee or pay for groceries, I usually follow a routine.

Clerk or barista: "Hello, how are you today?"

Me: "I feel fantastic! How is your day going?"

Clerk or barista (with a note of curiosity and enthusiasm): "Great, thank you!"

This simple conversation gets the person engaged beyond just processing your order. Baristas work hard, and in most cases, any "Thank you" they receive is for the change and receipt they give you. Did you notice the difference from the usual "Hello...fine thanks" or "not bad," or the blasé "okay?" If you really want to shake up your day, then be Remarkable in how you meet and interact with people. You may get some odd stares. However, in most cases, if you amp it up just a bit, you will lift others from their usual solemn, canned, and reactionary interactions.

Yes, this kind of interaction will require you to be more "on" than you're used to being, but it is so worth it! Besides, how's your current level of energy and enthusiasm working for you? When it comes to energy, like attracts like. So just a slight increase in your energy when you interact with others will create a tremendous spillover effect that will influence you in ways you cannot imagine.

Courage is the cement of the Remarkable Man's foundation. I know life can get hard, and at times, it feels like the walls are closing in on you. You may get to a place where you feel abandoned by those who should be supporting you. It may seem as though you have nowhere to turn. I'm here to tell you that you do have a place to turn. It starts by putting yourself in front of a mirror and getting real with where you are.

You have to summon courage to get to a place where you can be objective. Take a long look at your life. See all the components that make up your current circumstances. Remember, you put yourself in this situation. No one is to blame; no one is responsible but you. With that clear, it is up to you to muster the courage to make some changes. Don't worry; you already have the courage you need! You've had it before, so you can't say it doesn't exist. You just need to build up your "courage muscle."

Courage is not short-lived and measured in the number of deeds you accomplish. It's a way of living. It takes courage to get up and get to the gym every morning at six o'clock. It takes courage to refuse to spoil your kids. It takes courage to get back into the game after recovering from an injury. It takes courage to approach a beautiful woman and say hello. It takes courage to be a Remarkable Man in a changing world. And it takes real courage to take responsibility for your life.

A Remarkable Man has courage for every moment of the day. For the most part, the world is not going to recognize your courage. Your self-satisfaction is about the only form of gratitude or praise you will get for making changes in your life. Once you have become what you desire on the inside, your outside world will follow and those who matter will recognize and appreciate your courage. But it starts with you.

One of the biggest challenges I faced was completing this book. Even though I knew that the entire Remarkable Man Project rested on its completion, I used every excuse in the world to procrastinate and delay writing. My biggest slowdown came when there were only a couple of chapters left to write. The closer I came to completion, the more I found ways to distract myself. If I were working on this book on my laptop in a coffee shop, I allowed Facebook and other social media to dictate the outcome of my writing time. I even kept my cell phone in easy view and reaching distance, and I responded like a Pavlovian dog every time the little red light signaled the arrival of a new text message. I found myself on tangents, surfing the web about topics completely unrelated to my book. Why was I so easily distracted? It's because I knew a massive life change would be upon me soon. Finishing this book would stretch my comfort zone into unknown territory. It also represented a code of conduct I had to be congruent with, 100 percent. Then the negative mind chatter would show up. You might think I would have been thrilled to be so close to finishing. Oh, no! Surprisingly enough, I would think, "Wow! I'm almost finished. Am I actually living my message? Am I truly show-ing up in every way in my life?" The answer was, "No." If I even had to ask the question, if I had any self-doubt or feelings of concern, then I was not truly showing up in my life.

I had to let go of this block. I had to rid myself of all the "stuff" that filled my head, the "what ifs," the "not good enoughs," and outcomes only the Universe could foresee. This great self-assessment came to me at just the right time. With only a chapter or two left to go, I had to summon the courage to get real about where I was. I had to dig deep into what I really wanted in my life. I saw the finish line, and just like a marathon runner, I found the courage, strength, and will to power through and finish strong.

No matter what you are doing, no matter what your circumstances, and in spite of any challenges you face, you have the ways and means to overcome all your adversity. A great saying I heard some time ago really brings the point home. *You will never achieve more than your self-image will allow.* That powerful statement should cause you to take a hard look at your life. With courage and determination, you can change your self-image in a heartbeat.

Make this chapter and section of this book work for you. How much courage will it take to become a Remarkable Man? Remember, this is *your* image of *you* being a Remarkable Man. What will it take to move your biggest block(s) to freedom? In this context, freedom can mean anything you want. Freedom to travel, freedom from financial concerns, freedom from a bad relationship, freedom from a work environment that no longer serves you, freedom from health issues, and freedom to love yourself like never before!

Take solace in remembering that the Universe only gives you as much as you can handle. You are more powerful than you can imagine. I encourage you to find a little bit of courage every day to change, correct, or empower yourself to make a difference. It will take you another step closer to being a Remarkable Man for your life, and for those you care about.

Courage is not the absence of fear. It is acting in spite of it.
— Mark Twain

PART FOUR

THE CONSCIOUS <u>MAN</u>IFESTO OF THE REMARKABLE MAN

CHAPTER TEN

WHERE'S THE MAN?

Masculinity is not something given to you, but something you gain. And you gain it by winning small battles with honor.
— Norman Mailer

I hope you've read the entire book up to this point. The "Essentials" are there for your growth as a man. However, I forgive you if you jumped to this part of the book, as it's where the rubber meets the road. Here is where we get into the truth of our reality and where we find ourselves in this rapidly changing world.

This section will be a bit controversial for some. Based on feedback I received from both men and women, it is going to be one heck of an awakening and celebration for men. Yes, this section is about celebrating the masculine, the champion, and the essence of who you are as a man. I am going to be brutally honest with you because you deserve it and you can take it.

If you are a woman and reading this, please note, you aren't the target audience. However, you'll still want to engage in this section fully. Not for what it is, but for what it is *not*. This section is focused on, and directed toward, men. It is for the guys you adore, respect, and admire, as well as those you loathe, despise, and want out of your life. The Conscious MANifesto focuses on creating the Remarkable Man you ache to have in your life.

The revelations and insights in this section are responsible for incredible transformation in my life. I was able to create the Remarkable Man within myself and become a champion in a way that created rapid changes in my interactions and relationships with both men and women.

Men, are you ready to be fully open to knowledge that will take you further in your relationships and interactions with women than ever before? Are you open to learning about an international movement that empowers you to be a champion in all you are? Then let's get started.

First, you need to understand a few things about why I created The Remarkable Man in this place and time. The Remarkable Man is *not* about:

- playing the victim...this is not an "Us against Them" or "he said/she said" debate

- pointing fingers or playing the blame game

- right or wrong, better or worse, or creating gender issues to make an issue deeper than it already is

- being a pick-up artist or using psychological manipulation

- being homophobic, we know every man is a Remarkable Man, regardless of orientation

The Remarkable Man *is* about:

- creating the Champion within so he can show up and be a champion to women

- discovering the power of both masculine and feminine energy

- harnessing and celebrating the true, natural male power that governs everything he does

- Being the best Dad and/or role model to the children in his life

- engaging and connecting with his brothers at deeper levels to enrich friendships and business relationships

Masculine and Feminine Energy. I'm going to bring you in on a theory of mine that may bend your mind a little. Do you agree that everything is energy? It's true; everything has an energy vibration. Thoughts, physical objects, light, and sound all vibrate at certain frequencies of energy. Everything also has a cycle of existence. My theory is that our earth is going through a new cycle. In fact, we are in that transition period now. Every 13,000 years, our planet transitions from masculine to feminine energy. If you go back thousands of years, you'll see that feminine power dominated many cultures. The goddess and the queen were revered and very much the rulers and stewards of humanity. Then the masculine cycle returned and men were the vehicle for the masculine to play out its role. Women have not fared so well during our most recent period.

However, the feminine energy is returning. The first wave happened with the Suffragist Movement, allowing women to vote. Then a second wave hit. Interestingly enough, masculine energy counters these energy waves with violence to take control and we've had world wars to show for it. Women worked in factories while men went to blow each other up. When the men returned from war, they found different, more empowered women. The "Career Girl" was born. The third wave hit, and the feminist movement was fully out in the open. The "Age of Aquarius" is not just a hippie song from the '60s. No, it heralds the time of transition from the masculine to the feminine. We are in the last phase of transition. By the mid '90s, something huge occurred; the Internet went around the world and was fully accessible by almost anyone with a computer and a modem. Interestingly enough, women used it as a tool to unite, connect, and support one another. Most men used it to disconnect, tune out, and isolate themselves.

As a new millennium begins, the feminine energy continues to increase and more women feel a sense of being unstoppable. Men begin to languish. Unknowingly, something bigger is happening. Almost overnight, there's been a shift and the dynamics of relationships have changed. Men feel the shift, yet they have no idea it's happening. The statistics are staggering. Men between the ages of eighteen and forty-four are committing suicide in epidemic portions. Alcohol and drug abuse is out of control. College and university enrollment for men is at the lowest level in history. Guys, whether or not you agree with my theory, something big is happening and you cannot ignore it. Men are losing their masculinity and sense of self faster than you can imagine. Pay attention to this situation because it's global. You can feel it.

There is much to be said about women's progress over the last forty years. It is truly inspiring and honorable. Many people, both men and women, don't know that just a few decades ago, women in most of the world were not allowed to vote. Women were considered second-class citizens. In some cultures, they still are. Generations of courageous women fought a Draconian system to take their rightful place as equals with men. Yes, some areas still need improving. We won't even talk about the atrocities still being committed against women in some countries today.

As much as the Women's Movement created more equality for women, the pendulum has shifted for men. This pendulum swing has created confusion, frustration, and a bias regarding men. There are some great examples of this shift in pop culture today. In TV comedy today, men appear as imbeciles, goofballs, and chumps. Most family comedy shows have the mother as reasonably attractive (I'm being subjective), smart, and the common sense of the family. On the other hand, the man or husband is portrayed as somewhat unattractive, simple, helpless, and a poor role model to his children. In fact, his wife treats him as though he's just another kid. The male lead is constantly emasculated by his female counterpart. This is a proven comedy model that works for laughs and ratings today. Now think about TV commercials; here the man is using the inferior product, looking ridiculous and helpless—and the woman comes to the rescue, looking stunning, with the superior product. Again, this formula works because the commercials are geared toward a predominantly female buying public.

Think about a show or TV commercial that depicts the woman as comic relief and the man is in control. You can't, can you? That formula would never work in our society. Yes, many shows depict men and women as equally inept or unempowered, but not one shows a woman as less than a man.

I bring this matter to your attention and give you Homer Simpson (*The Simpsons*), Peter Griffin (*Family Guy*), and Raymond Barone (*Everybody Loves Raymond*) as examples of men depicted as idiots in the family dynamic. They're guys who, along with their goofball friends, can't seem to do anything right. With our pop culture generating the male image like this ad nauseam, it is hard to see men in the proper light.

The man vs. woman debate is fraught with misunderstandings and generalizations that consistently pull at our relationships due to the underlying way we view one another. Women roll their eyes at "typical male" behavior and men hit their heads against a wall, saying, "I don't understand her."

As I was writing this book, I looked for quotes about empowering men. What came up in my online search was startling. Out of 200 or so quotes, only eight were positive about men. The other 192 were scathing, sarcastic, insulting quotes, and primarily from women. Most were about our usefulness or lack thereof, or how simple and predictable we are. Quite sad, really.

Gentlemen, I wrote this book so we can lift this stigma and reclaim our authentic male power. We will lose our grip on the evolutionary ladder if we do not pay attention to what is going on out there. Here's a bit of truth you need to understand fully to empower yourself as a man. You must open your mind for this truth. Every preceding chapter gave you the tools and techniques to be a Remarkable Man. But more than that, what you've read was to help you trust me so I could share the truth with you. I hope you'll get this truth and believe what I tell you.

We live in a world of duality. Day and night, light, dark, up and down, and so on. The most obvious duality in our human experience is that of male and female. If I gave you two cards with the word "Masculine" printed on one and "Feminine" printed on the other, and asked you to put the appropriate card on a man and a woman sitting in a room, ten times out of ten, the masculine card would go to the man and the feminine card would go to the woman. However, masculine and feminine energy is bigger than any man or woman, and it has very little to do with gender. Listen to me now. As men, we have both masculine and feminine energy in us!

There, I said it. How's your ego doing? Just breathe. Come on, breathe. It's true...you have both masculine and feminine energy. I am not making this up. It is a scientific, Universal, and all-too-human truth. It is the Yin and Yang within us all. Relax! It doesn't mean you're gay! And if you are gay, then that's perfect for your life's experience. As Remarkable Men, we are all brothers.

As a man, you are primarily masculine, and most women are primarily feminine. When these energies cross, things get messed up. And messed up they are! These energies also govern our world, and feminine energy is now coming into a dominant cycle. With the cycle shifting, both males and females are being tested at a tremendous rate. This testing creates chaos, confusion, and frustration on many levels. What's happening on the spiritual level is an integration of masculine and feminine energy. Not male and female gender attributes, but the energies we share. We are moving toward wholeness, albeit kicking and screaming. This is our destiny as we evolve to higher levels of awareness. The challenge is that very few people have reached a level of awareness to appreciate this shift. It may take quite some time.

Few of us can claim to possess a balance of masculine and feminine energy. Yes, many "spiritual" folks claim to have it, but they don't truly embody that power. I can't add my name to the list that says I have balanced energy. I understand it theoretically and in my meditations, but I struggle with the delicate dance and power that it wields in our 3-D world. Because of this struggle, and because most of the population is unaware of the balance we are striving for, I am going to focus on the masculine and feminine energies as they are today and what that means to you as a man right here, right now.

Women are evolving at a tremendous rate. It is just how their feminine energy is wired. They have been on a quest for generations to feel their power in every sense of the word. We hear terms such as "Goddess," "Sisterhood," "Soul Sister," and so on. No matter where you are, women gather and support each other in countless women's groups. There are women's groups for business, fitness, personal growth, spirituality, readers, yoga, pregnancy, and much more. Many of these are international organizations. There are days on the calendar that celebrate women for any number of reasons.

So the question I pose to you is: How many men's groups do you know about? Seriously, when it comes to men's groups, how many can you recall? Yes, I remember the days of yesteryear when the elite and powerful had private "men-only" clubs. I'm sure they still exist in some form, but for the most part, they died out in the last two decades or so. You could argue that members of the Freemasons, Elks, Lions, and Rotary are primarily male. However, they aren't the kinds of groups we'd compare to the women's groups of today.

Most men's groups today (at least those I know about) are men's support groups. Images of drumming naked in the forest around a campfire come to mind. Or groups that meet in library basements where the discussion centers on the victim within. Many such groups do more harm than good to the fragile fabric between men and women. There's hardly any sense of long-lasting empowerment, community, or growth.

Men, we are falling behind in our evolution in many ways. The Remarkable Man is here to help us reclaim our authentic masculinity and celebrate, without apology, what it means to be Remarkable at this place in time.

Let's look at how masculine and feminine energies show up in our lives. A woman could be a great mother and wife/partner, nurturing, attentive to your needs, and obviously very much in her femininity. However, her day job may require her to be more masculine. She's a role model, a leader, a creative dynamo. Masculine energy is more helpful there for her to be effective.

A man could be powerful, strong, assertive, and very much in his masculine energy, but when he holds his baby girl in his arms, his feminine energy shines through. Do you see where I'm going with this? Your understanding of these energies is going to help your reclaim your power in an honorable, respectful, and rewarding way.

I am a perfect example in that I had to deal with a dynamic that showed me, full circle, the power in what I'm talking about. In my last serious relationship (we were engaged), I saw how the energies that brought us together also broke us apart. I also recognized patterns that had repeated throughout my life to enhance or destroy my relationships.

I met my then-fiancée when I was at the top of my game. My upstart media company was on the verge of tremendous success. I had all the trappings of a man on the rise. She was quite attracted to me because I represented the balanced alpha male she desired. She was successful herself, and was both Mom and Dad to her two preteen daughters. She worked in the very male-dominated world of investment financing.

The relationship was pure gold, with both romance and passion. I was the good male role model the girls needed, and it was a delight to be that for them. So it was easy for us to decide to get married. However, shortly after our engagement, the wheels began to fall off. As I shared earlier, the company I'd been so proud of was involved in a proxy battle that took the wind out of my sails, both emotionally and financially.

Of course, during this time I also learned that my son wasn't mine. This confident, powerhouse of a man was letting go of his masculinity day by day, and a feminine energy began to take over. I wanted to be nurtured and supported. We were living together and I spent more time at home, taking care of the house, while she was off making connections and closing deals.

We began to argue over little things, and I found myself feeling less of a man. I wanted to be in my own space a lot of the time. I was struggling with mild depression too, but I didn't know it at the time. On the surface, we looked like a great couple, just experiencing a few bumps along the way. However, not understanding how the masculine and feminine energies were playing a role in our lives would lead to the demise of our relationship.

You see, she'd had to play in the masculine world most of her life. She'd never really had a positive male role model. She longed to surrender that role to a man who could hold the masculine energy enough that she could surrender it and fully embrace her femininity. It's quite remarkable to see a woman who really embraces her feminine energy. However, due to my reversal of fortune, I'd lost a great deal of my masculine power. She began to wonder why she didn't find me as attractive as she once had. When you're in a relationship, nothing is worse than knowing and feeling she doesn't find you attractive like she once did. Yes, I was still good to her and a great father figure to her girls, but things were amiss. I began to resent her due to my insecurities. I wanted my power back, but she had it because I'd given it to her! I felt weak and out of sync with the world.

Gentlemen, you need to know something very important. Feminine energy is stronger than masculine energy. It has nothing to do with physical strength. Countless studies have shown that the feminine energy is stronger. This energy easily transfers to men. Again, I am not talking about making you less of a man, but if you are struggling to have more control of your life, you may want to take a hard look at this truth and decide how much you may be living from your masculine or feminine energy.

In my situation, my former fiancée longed to come home to the strong, powerful man I once was. She wanted to unload the masculine energy she'd worked with all day and surrender to my masculinity—an energy I was losing because, at a subconscious level, I allowed it to happen. We slowly drifted apart. I did what most men do when we feel things aren't going the way they should in a relationship. I started buying flowers and little gifts, being Mr. Nice Guy. As much as movies and pop culture want you to believe it, *this will not work unless you're in your masculine power.* Read that again! In fact, it can be sickly sweet and lead to a gag reflex in your partner. You are showing her your wussy self. Gifts and sweet nothings cannot take the place of a man being a champion in his authentic masculine power. That's what she really wants.

When I knew the relationship as I knew it was over, I blamed her for not being the woman I wanted her to be. I wanted a feminine woman, not a masculine one. So we were at a stalemate and didn't understand how we'd gotten there or how to fix it. We'd switched polarities and didn't even know it.

Our relationship as an engaged couple ended and we became just friends. For many men, this transition is very hard because it feels like the consolation prize. However, remember the reason, season, and lifetime aspects of why we draw people into our lives. In my case, she was the catalyst to help me remove the blinders and see the truth of whom I'd become.

Understanding my patterns, and how they played out, was crucial to my evolution. I began to see how this imbalance played a role in virtually every relationship I had been in. I'd start strong, and once the relationship was solid, my feminine self would surface to the point where I was not in my power. Through hindsight, I was able to study this duality and energy transfer. I realized my behavior and experience in relationships was not unique. I soon found that many men and women feel the same energy imbalances. As it turns out, almost everyone I talked to could not believe how accurately I described what they were feeling or experiencing in their lives and relationships. So I began my quest to research, study, and practice what I was discovering. I knew that men needed to return to their authentic masculine power, not only for themselves, but to be champions for their women too.

How the Masculine Serves You. Have you ever wondered why some men just seem to have it going on? When they walk into a room, their charisma fills the place. They're not always the most attractive guys in the room, but they have a certain energy that women love. This charisma is the result of masculine energy being in its rightful place, combined with knowing one's self.

Okay, guys, I don't mean to harp on the masculine and feminine energy concept, but if you truly get a grip on how it plays a role in your life, you will be able to empower your life to a degree you never thought possible. As a man, it is imperative that you embrace your masculine energy and understand its power. Don't apologize for this energy, either. Many people say we are moving toward the feminine energy, and men must bring it into their lives in order to bring love, balance, and harmony to the world. Men constantly hear that many of the world's ills throughout history were the product of man and his ego-driven masculine energy. Indeed, war, violence, greed, and political power are products of masculine energy. However, it doesn't mean these events are your fault because you're a man. There is perfection in the Universe. Everything is as it should be, and it always has been that way. I, by no means, endorse or accept the atrocities committed by the masculine energy. As a recovered conspiracist, I know very intimate details about the power elite and the "master plan" on this earth. The control mechanism is very powerful and convincing. However, as in everything, the hold ego has had on the masculine energy cycle is ending, and the world is moving toward the feminine cycle. As shown in the Vesica Pisces symbol below, humanity is in transition right now.

During this transition, men can take on more authentic and empowered roles. You're a man, and the term "man up" is appropriate in the context of becoming a Remarkable Man. There will be no talk here of diminishing your power as a man. In fact, quite the opposite is true. With this book, I hope to be a catalyst for change, to get rid of the old-world masculine where the ego is in power, and bring forth authentic masculine power that honors and respects the true essence of a woman, brings you confidence and creativity, and gives you inner knowledge of who you truly are.

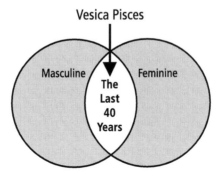

Think about the arguments you've had in relationships, both current and past. Chances are you were in your feminine energy and she was in her masculine. Or you were in your *ego* masculine. *Ego* masculine is about being right; you have something to prove. Both men and women share this component. Rarely is an argument about the subject at hand. It's usually about an underlying issue that isn't being addressed. In many cases, the reason is not even known at a conscious level. Why do you think you don't understand women at times? Why do you feel that some arguments don't make sense? It is due to a lack of awareness of the energies and polarities that have switched around on us.

What are your habitual argument or conflict patterns with your wife, girlfriend, or partner? Be honest here. Do you block and not let her finish her point? Do you leave the room? Do you have a temper? Do you become quiet? These are all aspects of the self you need to explore. What are your triggers? Are they patterns in keeping with a masculine energy or a feminine energy? There's no right or wrong here. These are just some behaviors to observe as you show up when it truly matters.

A masculine man is attractive and in short supply, according to most women. There was a time when people believed women wanted the SNAG (Sensitive, New Age Guy). You could go through hundreds of dating sites and read ads from women who wanted a sensitive, awake man who really "gets her." That might be great in the short-term, but after a while, the balance of energy would shift and she'd wonder why she was no longer attracted to him. He wouldn't have the power he needs to be a champion in her life for the long haul. Mr. Sensitive New Age Guy probably isn't having much luck outside his circle of influence either.

I played the SNAG role for a while, and I thought it would work. I thought it was what women wanted. There were women I wanted to be with sexually, but they just wanted to be my friend because I was nice and could have deep conversations. It really sucks to be a girl's "buddy" when you're physically attracted to her. Do you know what

I mean?

Let's look at the flipside of the "Nice Guy." Here is where the "Bad Boy" enters the scene. Many men have adjusted their world through personal growth and self-development. They figure they've become the well-adjusted, kind, and gentle man for whom most women are looking. But then, women leave them for a "wild man," or "bad-boy" type. You know what I'm talking about. A woman will seek this bad boy, even at the risk of losing her relationship or way of life, mostly because she doesn't know how to fix it or when it's time to leave. Her man is not showing up the way she envisioned, but she loves him and doesn't want to hurt him. She's not "in lust" anymore and wants her man to take on more of the masculine energy to bring back that spark. That spark may never reignite if the man doesn't know he has moved more into his feminine energy. To the woman, subconsciously, if she has an affair, the risk of being caught is worth it. The truth of her feelings and frustrations will be the "out" she hasn't had the courage or understanding to express.

You've probably had similar scenarios in your life when you continue on a path that does not serve you. The Universe sends you an experience to shake up your world, sometimes very dramatically, to get you to change direction. An affair is one of those scenarios. In most cases, it marks the beginning of the end of a relationship that a woman is too afraid to end on her own. Many of us would never act on the impulse to have an affair, but if we're honest with ourselves, we'll admit that the thought has entered our mind. I'm proud to say I've never cheated, but I will be honest and say I've been tempted many times.

I live in a city where the divorce rate is about 70 percent. That's not a typo. Yes, 70 percent is incredibly high and does not bode well for the institution of marriage. I can count on one hand the number of happy marriages I am aware of. I have admired people for modeling what a great marriage and relationship should look like, only to find out that they've recently separated and divorce is the next step.

The average new marriage now begins to fall apart in just four years, even sooner for common law relationships. Why is coupling becoming such a challenge? I believe it is due to the evolution and awakening of a sense of self that is stronger now than it's ever been. Because of this awareness, the weaker reasons for getting into a long-term, committed relationship are falling away. Weaker reasons like: codependency, neediness, and fear of being alone. Many people, if they were honest with themselves, would admit they want someone in their life in order to have a witness. In other words, we want to go through life with someone to share our experiences, triumphs, sadness, and joy. Going through life without someone there to witness it seems a little empty. Or at least it did. Now people are evolving into their individuality. The "need" to be with someone is shifting to a "want," and an option to being single. However, being single has changed dramatically too and is a preferred lifestyle for many. Being single no longer carries the stigma it once did. When I was young, if you were a divorcee or a bachelor, it meant you slept around and/or nobody wanted you. Thank God, times have changed!

In today's environment, it's acceptable to say, "If I leave you, I'll be okay. I'll do just fine without you." This is the new reality of relationships. You cannot pretend it is not there. People have options and act on them more and more. You have to get wise about something very real. Today, women see many examples of the powerful single woman who's living life on her own terms and having a lot of fun doing it. All those women's groups have an impact in their lives. Women even celebrate their newfound singleness with divorce parties. How many men do you know who do the same thing?

Men rarely celebrate the loss of a relationship. It means we failed at something and we'd rather keep it to ourselves. We feel a sense of shame, and shame is kryptonite to men. Shame a man and he is down for the count. Yes, women know about this weakness in our armor too!

As women connect, grow, and evolve, doesn't it make sense that they're raising the bar for the type of men they want in their lives? Of course, it does, but due to how our society is built, few men are around to meet these new and demanding standards.

Due to past hurts, you might have a school of thought that says, "Fuck 'em!" Why the hell do I have to change?" Well, this is not about "Us and Them." This is about you moving beyond the self to something bigger. It's about taking your authentic masculine energy to a whole new level.

Guys, I'm telling you this because if you aren't aware of the rapidly changing relationship environment, and why women are becoming more selective in the type of man they want, you need to wake up—fast! Unless you've been living under a rock and haven't noticed, women have options. If you think you're "all that" in bed, apparently you haven't heard of Mr. Rabbit, Mr. Bullet, Mr. Wonderful, or whatever women call their toys. Additionally, a woman would rather be single than be with a guy she views as not evolved or out of sync with his masculine power. And don't think for a moment that you're excused from making a change because you're married or in a long-term relationship. She has, is, or has already thought about leaving your ass! She's just waiting for one more screw-up from you or one more lame excuse. If you want your relationship to last, you don't have the option to coast through it and run it on autopilot anymore!

CHAPTER ELEVEN

THE REMARKABLE MAN

Successful relationships don't just happen out of nowhere...
they take time, commitment, faith,
and two people that honestly want to be together.
— DeAndre Carswell

The Remarkable Man is the type of man who will achieve success in this new world of relationships. I am not in any way making this discussion all about women and the power they hold over you. As I said, we aren't trying to create an "Us vs. Them" energy here. I can appreciate that it could easily go that way for many of you. However, I am revealing a truth you must understand if you are to have success in your relationships and interactions with women.

How can you become a Remarkable Man in this new world of relationships? It's not that difficult; it just requires you to awaken to the truth of who and what you are. You are a Remarkable Man right now! I mean it in every sense of the word. Whatever names, labels, or categories you may have given yourself before, you have the ability to rise above them and claim your true champion power.

Remember the reference to the "Bad Boy" women seem to desire? In truth, that persona is only sustained for a short while, as the masculine is too strong, one-dimensional, and is usually based in ego. This persona can also be very destructive and abusive. Women, it may seem like he has it all together, but he's not the man you think you want him to be. We'll get to that soon.

The Sexy Vixen is similar to the Bad Boy. She's hot and passionate. She's your fantasy woman, but she might not be able to communicate at your level. Yes, the sex is great (possibly not), she looks great on your arm, and your buddies eat it up. Over time though, you will want more than she may be capable of giving.

The Tomboy Type is desirable if you are a sports or outdoorsy type. She's lots of fun and can hold her own with the boys. But you may long for her to put away her sweats and running shoes and put on her little black dress and heels and be the lady you desire. In the beginning, these scenarios are exactly what you want. Time is the true test and the relationship is most likely doomed to fail if you want more than she's prepared to give.

In a Bad Boy, the ego typically will be the controlling energy. Let's examine the Bad Boy's magnetic attraction, since many men wish they could embody these characteristics at some level themselves. Let's look at the best of the Bad Boy's energy. This energy is what most women crave and lust after, even if they never admit or follow through on it. When I use the term "Bad Boy," it doesn't mean I am always referring to the hard-edged macho jerk or asshole. He can be an average looking guy who is confident and charismatic and just knows who he is. Most women will say they don't desire any aspect of this guy, but the multi-billion dollar romance novel industry proves otherwise. The Bad Boy's energy allows a woman to surrender much of the masculine within and embrace her feminine energy for her man. There's an important point here. Drop the ego! The Bad Boy is not who or what you want to be. We are going for the champion here, The Remarkable Man—not a conqueror of feelings and emotions. The Bad Boy exemplifies one thing: he's confident (arrogant, in most cases) and he knows it. That's what she wants (at least aspects of it). She wants a man who knows who he is, what he wants, and how to go after it. She wants to feel that strength within you.

So from here, how will you get that inner strength? How will you get the confidence? The only way you can get these qualities is through practice. You become confident through experience. Having the same experience repeatedly and making the right course corrections each time will help you overcome your nervousness or uncertainty because you've done it before and won.

You have to get out into the world that you want to own. If you long to be a champion for your wife, girlfriend, or companion, then become one! Look at romantic movies. In most, the couple faces some sort of challenge they have to overcome. In the end, the male lead usually has to deal with his insecurities and rise to the challenge. He gets the girl and he loses the girl. Then, he becomes a Remarkable Man and finds her again. In most cases, the guy is just an average Joe, but he becomes larger than life to get the girl of his dreams. It's a formula that works for millions of female movie fans. It will work for you. Start today and show up for her like you've never done before. Understand how strong you truly are. You are a magnificent man. Breathe *that* in!

You will need to practice being stronger in who you are. I'm talking about inner strength. Your looks have nothing to do with your magnetism. Yes, it helps to look your best, and I encourage you to make that a part of your daily ritual. Women appreciate the little details. However, it's just a small part of the picture. In truth, women are attracted to your energy. What's going on inside you will show on the outside. However, nothing will change until you do!

CHAPTER TWELVE

MALE STATUS

*The activities we observe in the outer world are but typical of that
which is taking place in man's inner world of thought and feeling.*
— Charles Patterson

Remember when I told you about my fight with Chief when I was
fifteen years old? Before that fight, my reputation was that of a wimp,
a loser, and I was invisible to most people. Then I won the fight and
something happened. People noticed me. The cool kids wanted to
hang out with me and girls flirted with me. What happened? It's
simple; in those few moments, I gained status. My status in the herd,
if you will, rose to the point that people noticed me. This is an interesting dynamic in human behavior. People are attracted to those
who have status.

You don't have to be rich, famous, or have all the toys in order to have
status. I'm not talking about titles or position, either. You just have to
own who you are and make the best of what you have. Think about
it. Artists, poets, or musicians may not have much money at all. Yet
you see them with beautiful women all the time. Why? Because they
have status based on their passion and knowing who they are. They
make no apologies for where they are in life. You have to accept them
on their own terms. Many women find this romantic and sexy. Is status enough to maintain a long-lasting relationship? The "struggling
artist" phase can get old fast, but if both are happy with what they
give each other, status really doesn't matter.

When a man walks into a room and a woman pays attention, it's because he has status and she likes the way it looks on him. You don't need an entourage of friends to prove you have status, either. Just be mindful of your physiology, how you hold yourself, and how you move. Be aware of your breathing too...slow it down. Status is also created by how you engage others in conversation. You have to get involved in the discussion. Raise a few points of your own and back them up.

Women can sense status, but men can sense it too. You see it all the time in meetings and gatherings, where one or two men have the dominant energies. I don't mean men who are all bravado, attention whores, and show-offs. I'm talking about men who really own their space. Men who are calm, cool, and make great eye contact. You like them, but they also intimidate you. You're intimidated because these men know themselves—and you—better than you do. Get that inner game going for yourself; it's imperative to becoming a Remarkable Man.

After my break-up, I resisted the singles scene for several months. Then one night, I went with some friends to our favorite pub. It is usually full of beautiful women. That night was no exception. I've always had fun in social settings. I enjoy meeting new people and can hold my own in most any dynamic. I'm in good shape at 6' 4" and up on men's fashions, so you'd think I was successful in chatting with the ladies on that particular night. Not only did I *not* chat with the ladies, but not one woman came over to me. I felt like no one even noticed me. Even when I tried to strike up a conversation, I fell flat and everything seemed forced and awkward. On the other hand, my two friends are average in looks, and they didn't look particularly stylish that night. Yet both ended up chatting and laughing with the ladies. One actually got a phone number and a date! This is a good example to show that your outer façade has little impact when it comes to a woman's attraction to you.

What did my friends have that I *didn't* have that night? I was carrying a lot of mental baggage with me. I was not myself on the inside, and that's what I conveyed on the outside. My self-confidence was low and I was somewhat needy. I was aligning more with my small self and it showed. There was no status at all coming from me. My inner self was more the wussy, little boy energy that I hated within myself. How could a woman find that remotely attractive? Yuck!

I needed to dig deep into the masculine man I really was. He was there, buried somewhere, but I had forgotten him. This wake-up call told me I had to work in order to get back to where I'd been before. I wouldn't be able to change my reality until I gave up my story of being small. I'd had enough and wanted to know why I was the way I was. I studied human psychology and behavior, and I got into books and programs that went deep into why we do what we do. I was online constantly, reading and listening to the latest "guru-speak" on the subject. However, my world did not change, even after I'd read all the material available to help me. The reason? I did not take action right away. When I finally went out and practiced what I'd learned, it began to sink in and take hold. The light switch went on and I began to see some dramatic improvements. This stuff works! I started to look at every aspect of my life where I was not being Remarkable and made course corrections from there.

The Remarkable Man was someone I longed to become. I wanted to be "that guy" who makes a positive impact in people's lives. I wanted to bring out the happy, outgoing, and courageous man within me. I wanted to be around beautiful, talented women. I wanted to be around charismatic, successful men. As James Allen said, "You do not get what you want; you get what you are." Well, I wanted to get much more than who and what I was. I wish I could tell you there's a miracle cure and you'll change overnight. That's not what this book is about.

Being a champion for your relationships, dating, marriage, and most importantly, yourself can only come with educating yourself and taking action. It just doesn't happen overnight. Nothing is going to change unless you make change a priority. Understanding the balance of masculine and feminine energy is the key to your success. Master this and you'll be on your way to becoming The Remarkable Man you know you can be.

CHAPTER THIRTEEN

THE MASCULINE/FEMININE (UN)BALANCE

Let's look at a few areas where you can start to make some positive changes in your life.

If you truly want to be a champion and be a Remarkable Man in every sense of the word...then you must get clear on where you are right now. If you were honest with yourself, where would you say your masculine/feminine balance is today?

I want to reiterate that feminine and masculine energy have nothing to do with gender. Yes, we understand traditional male/female roles. However, we all have both energies. For those who are uncomfortable with this idea or admitting it's possible, the truth is feminine energy is stronger than masculine energy. Let's clarify. Feminine energy is nurturing, loving, intuitive, and compassionate. Our planet's entire power source is creative, feminine energy. This energy is to be honored and respected.

I'll be very clear here and state that masculine and feminine energy *cannot* be in balance in today's world. As a species, we are not ready for perfect balance. We can pretend we are, but very few people have reached the state of awareness to live it. Humanity just hasn't evolved to that level of consciousness. We live in a world where that utopian concept is still a few years away. For our purposes in The Remarkable Man philosophy, we say that for a man to step into his Remarkable power, he should strive for 70 percent authentic masculine energy and about 30 percent feminine energy. Women should strive for 70 percent feminine energy and 30 percent masculine energy. If men are more than 70 percent masculine, they have a tendency to go toward the ego-centered, masculine energy, and that's not what we're about. If we go too far to the feminine, we lose our sense of self, and most women won't find the natural attraction for which they're looking.

Obviously, relationship dynamics exist where the masculine/feminine energy is more neutral. Bravo! It works for some. I am not saying it doesn't. However, for the bulk of the population, this is not the case and the divorce/relationship statistics back it up.

The feminine energy is stronger than the masculine in many ways. You see this when a woman uses her feminine charms. She can cause many a man to give away his power in a heartbeat. I'll go into this shortly. The masculine can be tamed very easily.

When a well-dressed, confident, feminine woman walks down the street and passes a construction site with ego-driven, masculine men, whistling and cheering are ways they typically show their gender and the energy they have. In this example, who do you think holds the power? You guessed it. As in most cases, the feminine energy is in power. Feminine power is usually quite stable and continuous. Masculine power often needs to be pumped up, rallied, and energized.

No matter where you think you are and where you know you are on the scale, it is critical to understand how these energies play out and cause the experiences you have. You must understand where you are with your energy. You must be able to observe a situation and ask yourself, "Who am I right now? Am I more masculine or feminine right now? What would best serve the purpose in this situation?"

When you aren't moving forward with what you want, you're probably too much in your feminine energy—out of sync with what you need. I'm not referring to puffed-up, ego-driven masculine energy. I'm talking about a poised, unapologetic, male confidence that comes from deep within and knowing who you are. From here, you are in control of your world. Most women want this man. They don't want someone who always agrees with them, someone who fawns and gushes over them, or someone who puts them on a pedestal. She does not want you to look up to her! She wants to look up to you! She wants to feel weak in your arms; she wants to feel your energy that says you are in control and that she is safe and secure. Yes, money, looks, and prestige get a lot of attention when it comes to what we *think* a woman wants in a man, but it really comes down to her inner sense that you are the guy she is both challenged by and enamored with.

Being Remarkable in your relationships takes effort by both parties. We must understand why relationships break down the way they do, sometimes before they even get started. Women have a responsibility in their roles too. However, it is more complicated to understand. A woman in her masculine energy can often be attractive. The masculine shows up in her business sense, her decisiveness, and her control of her world. Yet that power is seldom attractive to men.

I know many successful women who are at the top of the game in the business world only to be weak in the relationship world. A large part of this situation is due to the intimidation factor perceived by men. Yes, most men think they can handle a strong, assertive woman. However, unless he is at her "status" level or above, he will have a hard time understanding her world and may not have enough masculine power to allow her to let her masculine energy go. His insecurities begin to pop up. *Who is she meeting for that power lunch? Why does she have to work late? Did she have to wear that pencil skirt and heels today? With so many men attracted to her, she knows she can do better than me.*

At another level, most guys are visual creatures. So when we see a beautiful woman in a sexy, revealing outfit, we think, "Wow! That kind of woman turns me on. That's what I want in my life." Yeah, right! Your possessive insecurities will pop up faster than pimples on a teenager after a sugar binge.

The truth is, that sexy woman on your arm feels and looks great while you are in your authentic, masculine energy because you could not care less what people think or feel. You are proud and secure with who you are as a man. Here's a biggie: you also trust and respect your beautiful woman. When your authentic, masculine energy starts to wane, your insecurities will make you feel jealous and small. You'll want her to tone down the sexiness. When your masculine power diminishes and insecurities surface, you want to keep the beauty and sexiness to yourself. It could become all-consuming, especially if she is going to work or go out with friends. You think about all the other guys who will check her out and want her. You may become so obsessive and controlling in this manner that you begin to show your lack of power and control. It is important to remember why you wanted this sexy woman in the first place. Now that you have her, you want to change her. That won't work. In fact, it will drive her away. Your insecurities will end up as self-fulfilling prophecies.

A Remarkable Man is always in control and does not need to be worried, jealous, or controlling. Let her be the woman she is. Let her wear what works for her, no matter her body type or style. You can make suggestions about what you like to see on her, but if you do, err on the side of what makes *her* feel good, not what makes *you* feel good. In most cases, she will give you more than you ask for.

Now I know it would be only fair to address the ladies on this, right? It sometimes feels unfair that we men have to do all the changing. It seems like all the work and effort has to come from us, and the women have it easy. They get to sit back and enjoy the benefits of us owning our true power and becoming Remarkable Men. That's just bullshit and unfair, right? Well, gentleman, that's just the way it is! I know you were hoping I'd rally for you, jump up on my soapbox, and tell it to the ladies like it is. The truth is, I just did! Women have known all this on many levels for years. However, I'm putting a unique spin on the energy dynamics.

The reality is, if you rise up from the patterns that have destroyed or limited your relationships, and you become a true Remarkable Man, you will get a woman who will give tenfold what you give. It's true! Women are wired that way; they are natural givers. If you provide an environment that allows her to feel all she can, she will become the flower that grows, buds, and blossoms in brilliant colors because you provided the care, strength, and support for her to do so. You'll get your best friend, your faithful soul mate, your passionate lover, and your fantasy girl. With your energy, you can manifest her through the way you treat her. You can read all the relationship books in the world, but it doesn't work the other way around. It's like gravity. You can't fight it...it's the law.

If you are a woman reading this chapter, then you know I'm close on this one. I have identified exactly what you have experienced in relationships most of your life. You may not agree with me or subscribe to how I have outlined the masculine and feminine energy game, but you know the truth. You understand how powerful men would be if they understood and applied this awareness in their lives. Yes, you'd have a Remarkable Man in your life.

This chapter is not all about men changing all they know and who they are to please women. Not in the least. There needs to be some give and take here. You also need to be aware that women also have energy imbalances. Women must take responsibility for being able to recognize when you're too much in the masculine. Yes, you hold more masculine energy today than ever before. In order for you to play at a high level in this world, you have to be in your masculine energy to be effective. Carry *this* energy into your relationships and interactions with men. When challenges arise and you are not feeling the love in your relationship, ask yourself, "Where am I in my energy?"

Women, what, if anything, have you done to take away your man's masculine energy? I'm serious! Take a good look at where and when the energies may have shifted in your relationships. What happened? What set of circumstances occurred to cause the man to whom you were so attracted to change? When did his inner "wuss" or "little boy" show up? When did your feminine energy change for him? I ask these questions only because it is easier for women to be in their masculine energy than it is for men to be in theirs. It's true! Women can hold out longer than men can, and sex is often used as a bargaining chip. Women, because you're more aware of your feelings, your inner work is far less than it is for men. Societal norms have created this dynamic, and my perspective isn't going to change it one bit. However, I do hope to put out there a modicum of conscious, male energy that might prompt you to take another look at how you see the men in your life.

As a woman, you hold the power in most healthy relationships. You do in every sense of the word. As much as you want the man to have it, you hold the energy of the relationship. Men like to believe they have the relationship and family dynamic under their confident control, but *you* do! You can see evidence of this everywhere. Take product promotion, for example. Other than lawn care and big screen televisions, advertisers target most of their campaigns toward women because they know you make most of the buying decisions in your home.

The cheating husband is also less common than we've been led to believe. Contrary to pop culture, more women cheat in their relationships than men do. There's also the startling fact that 10 percent of men aren't the fathers of their children, and they don't even know it! In fact, in some U.S. states, the rate is more than 30 percent! By now, women should realize that their power has passed societal norms of the past. The "man of the house" status men once claimed doesn't have the teeth it once had.

Okay, back to you men. Don't feel sorry for women and let their claims of woe influence you. We should acknowledge and honor the work that women have done for the last 100 years to obtain their power and influence in the world. We also realize male/female roles and expectations aren't the same as they once were. In the western world, women control 60 percent of the wealth, make 85 percent of consumer purchases, bring 70 percent of divorce actions, and 90 percent of the time, they have custody of the children. It's indeed a different world. However, in this new environment, we can all enjoy fulfilling, passionate, and romantic relationships.

Women in most cases are automatically tuned into their feeling center. They operate from this place as a matter of course. Women can help their men become the Remarkable Men they desire by understanding their vibrational frequency. Is there room for him to take back his authentic power?

What needs to happen is men and women need to open each other's "owner's manual" and take the time to reevaluate where their energies are. Find out where those energies went and how to get them back into alignment so both are feeling that proper transfer of energies. Talk about what each of you needs from the other to feel the masculine and/or feminine energy you desire.

Our world is changing very rapidly and we really do need to come together and support and honor the masculine/feminine differences. Each will serve you well when the time is right. However, if you have been challenged with relationships, friendships, and interactions with others, there's a good chance these energies may be out of balance.

In order to be a Remarkable Man, you need to be clear about where you are in your relationships. If you're not where you want to be, change it! You can ask your partner, friends, and colleagues to give you an honest assessment of where you are, but intuitively, you already know.

For me, making the conscious decision to become a more masculine man was a process, a worthwhile life-changing shift. Today, I have my confidence back. I can talk with anyone, anywhere, and built rapport and connection with those I meet. I can read both male and female vibrational energy in people, and I know where they are based on their energy. Based on that, I can adjust my energy to match, off-set, or complement theirs. Through my own experiences and studies, I know that if men and women could understand their energies better, there would be less conflict and misunderstanding.

I don't mean to imply that this new level of awareness will assist those with deep emotional or mental challenges. If you find yourself in that scenario with a partner, then I suggest you ask yourself why you've put yourself in that situation. What's the payoff? What part of you has to learn from a person who will not or cannot respond to a new way of an authentic true connection? Remember why you manifested the people you have in your life.

As a Remarkable Man, you have to take responsibility for your energies. If you can't change yourself, don't try to fix someone else—it won't work! It is very difficult to use this technique with a person who is unwilling to be honest in who he is and what he really needs. *You* are the only person you have. If you have a hatred for women, homosexuals, or any other part of the population, then brother, you have a hatred for a part of yourself. Remember, everything that's happened to you was part of your learning experience. What role did you play in bringing it about? The more you protest, the more you need to look at your own challenges and behavior issues.

I'm sure this section hit hard for you in many ways. You know in your core that the information I'm presenting here is true. Many men and women have told me that the Remarkable Man theory is spot-on as to what they are experiencing in their relationships. They just didn't have the words or language to describe it.

So many women tell me that their men aren't the ones they fell in love with. His little-boy self, or inner wimp, has taken over and she is no longer attracted to him. In fact, one woman confided she was leaving her husband of many years and he couldn't do a thing to stop it. He tried everything—flowers, gifts, and counseling—but that just drove her further away. She was disgusted by his wimpiness and groveling. You see, she was bored. The routine lifestyle was not enough anymore. Yes, he was a good man, did everything to spoil her and be the man he thought she needed, but in the end, it was not enough. Now he's beside himself because he can't figure it out. He sees the world through the old paradigm, and it's eating him alive. The world is littered with men who are alone, bewildered, and confused as to why their wives, partners, or girlfriends left them or are about to leave.

If you find yourself in this scenario, I'm sorry, but for most of you, it's too late! I hate to be the bearer of bad news, but if she's on her way out, no amount of Remarkable Man behavior will change her mind at the eleventh hour. If you really want her back, you may have to let her go for a time. I know it hurts, but it takes time to switch to a Remarkable Man mindset and *then* convince her you're a new man. She still sees a wimp, so give her space to be alone. She'll see your Remarkable turnaround in time, but it has to come from an authentic place. She needs to feel your truth and *you* need to follow up with action. That doesn't mean calling her all the time, showering her with gifts, and doing her bidding. Those actions might be what caused the break-up in the first place! Be Remarkable in a powerful way by being the rudder and sails of your own ship. Once she sees you as commander-in-chief of your own life, you will become more attractive to her.

On the surface, this seems like a crazy amount of effort just to please women. Not at all. Imagine what your life would be if you were in control again, or for the first time. Imagine how every area of your life would change. All your interactions would improve. That's what this book is about: getting you to be your own person, a man who no longer needs approval or recognition from others. Let your attitude, deeds, and inner power reflect the way people see you.

We all want happiness in our relationships, but if we don't understand the concept of masculine and feminine energy, we'll end up in lackluster situations, and our happiness will be short lived. It's time to be the man you really are. It is the perfect barometer to measure the state of your relationship. If you can be real and objective about the reality you find yourself in, then you can learn to make adjustments that enhance your relationship like never before. You'll also recognize you deserve more and you'll have the strength to do something about it.

If you're in a relationship, focus on your commonalities. Get to the root of your real attraction. What are you both passionate about? What do both of you care about? I'm talking about things outside your relationship. There is where you rebuild the power and connection you once had. I want you to become a champion in her world and in your life. You can do that by taking control of the situation. Do not ask her where she wants to go to dinner or what activity she'd like to do. Just tell her this is what you're going to do. Obviously, consider what she enjoys. Telling her you're taking her to a tractor pull because you got free tickets is not going to excite her, unless she'd genuinely like that activity. Tell her you're taking her for a drive to a place you know would be an adventure for both of you. Talk, have fun, and explore. Shared experiences pull you closer. Yes, video night on the couch is great, but not every date night. A Remarkable Man keeps her guessing; he's unpredictable and thoughtful. Your memory of things that matter to her is more powerful than any bouquet of flowers or token gift. Call her and say, "I don't have much time, but I just want to let you know I'm thinking about you." Keep it short. Don't babble on. Say goodbye and get off the phone. If you get her voicemail, do the same thing. She'll feel great, enamored, and special. You have earned a gold star, and she'll look forward to your next call or get-together.

Let's take a moment to talk about gifts. Most men don't understand when it's right—or wrong—to give a gift. Again, this situation has a lot to do with our social conditioning. Contrary to popular belief, flowers, gifts, and expensive dinners do little to win her heart. In fact, the opposite often happens. It tells her that you are making up for your lack of imagination and masculine power by externalizing your feelings into objects. It's fine to give gifts and such on special occasions that warrant it. However, she needs to miss you too. Let some time go by; allow for the vessel between the two of you to fill over time, not all at once. If you are constantly trying to validate your role in the relationship, you have already lost, my brother.

Personally, I love to go out for dinner, no matter who I'm with. If I happen to dine with a beautiful date, then so much the better. Depending on your place in life, you'll find women who have certain expectations when they're dating. Going out for dinner is one of them. Just don't try to impress her with the expensive dinners all the time. You'll get more mileage from a walk in the park and then cooking together at your place. Save the expensive dinners for special occasions or celebrations. Be original and creative.

A Remarkable Man is a gentleman for a lady and a man for a woman. Knowing this truth can make amazing things happen. Be a consummate gentleman by opening her door; be attentive and strong, but do not fawn. Fawning gives away your power. Be decisive and just "be" with her. Don't ask her what she's thinking ten times a day. Do not ask where you stand in the relationship. That immediately says, "I'm insecure. I need to know you're not thinking bad things about me. Validate Me!"

Many men lose their power or give it away shortly after they get into a relationship. You stop seeing your friends and instead spend every waking moment with your new sweetheart. Then you begin to do her bidding. Your conditioning says this behavior is what you are supposed to do. There's no room here for push-pull sexual tension. You fill your vessel to overflowing in the first few months and brag to your buddies (when you make time for them) that you have a great relationship. Meanwhile, she's been giving her friends the "411" on you since the beginning. Very few women give up their friends when they begin a new relationship. "Girl time" is as vital to them as the blood that flows through them. She's telling them that, yes, you are a great guy. She tells them she loves you, but you don't have a backbone. You're sweet and do everything a good man should, but she's sick of it and longs for some Remarkable manliness and mystery. She doesn't want predictability. Most women don't brag about their guy with their friends. No detail escapes discussion. You become as intimately linked to her friends as you are to her. Yeah, they know about your Johnson and what it is—or isn't capable of doing for her. You know it!

Why do you ditch your friends for the new girl in your life? Almost every guy has done so at one time or another. Did she tell you what you could and couldn't do? Did she give you the feeling that if you went out with your friends, it meant you didn't care about her? It's sad to watch a man lose interest in his friends in what he thinks is a great move to solidify a relationship. I want to make this clear: there are great friends, and there are friends who aren't your friends; they're crabs in your bucket that will pull you down. If she's a bright girl and sees your potential, she will probably question your choice of friends. However, if you have good people in your life, it's imperative that you don't lose connection with them just because you're in a new relationship.

You need to be with your brothers once in awhile! You need to bond with your boys. It's healthy, it's fun, and it is allowed. Most women want their men to have their own world to play in—something that's his alone. If you're a family man, then obviously, your family comes first. As said in a previous chapter, children need to see their fathers hanging around with great friends. Remember, your friends are an extension of you. They're role models too.

CHAPTER FOURTEEN

SHOW HER YOUR AUTHENTIC POWER

What women want: To be loved, to be listened to, to be desired, to be respected, to be needed, to be trusted, and sometimes, just to be held. What men want: Tickets for the World Series.
— Dave Barry

The new authentic masculine man is ready to let go of his ego and the misconception that he has to "win," or prove something in every conflict. What you're arguing about is rarely the real issue, so let go of it. We no longer need to jump to our former knee-jerk reactions when we're in conflict with our partners. As Remarkable Men, we're strong and enlightened enough to know better. Remember this fact the next time you're in conflict with your partner. If you're single, your time will come, and you'll be glad you know this. Think of it this way: you can be smugly right or you can be peacefully happy.

The next time you and your partner are having a shouting match, or however you typically behave during conflict, I challenge you to shut your mouth. Don't say a word; just let her vent. Release your every urge to react. Yeah, you'll need to be a Remarkable Man to do so, but I know you can. Breathe deeply and fill your chest. Stand tall and hold your shoulders back. Breathe in your authentic masculine energy. Let it course through your veins, and fill your entire being with this power. Now understand something very important. She is not angry with you for the reason you *think* she's angry. I know it sounds strange, but it's true. Something's missing here, and you need to put the missing piece in place. What you are about to do will go against your programming in a big way. This process will challenge you like nothing before, but the rewards are astounding.

While she's standing there, upset and yelling at you, slowly walk toward her. Do not say a word, but express compassion, strength, and sincerity with your eyes. She may react negatively, and yell more, maybe even tell you to stay away from her. She says that because she sees a behavior pattern in you she's never seen before. Persist with your quiet strength and keep moving into her. She wants your strength, and she feels you now. She may even hit your chest or push you away. She's testing your strength and resolve. Are you as strong as you need to be? Now, without taking your eyes off hers, take her by the waist and pull her to you. Let her yell and be mad; you can take it. Don't say a word, but hold her and don't let go. Let your eyes be your method of communication. Look into her eyes with compassion and love. It is very important that you do not apologize. Don't pacify her or say what you think she wants to hear. You'll be wrong, anyway. Just hold her. As you do, the magic will begin. You may even feel a shift in energy with her immediately. Her energy needs a place to go. You were too much in your feminine and she was too much in her masculine. You need to provide the way for her to drop into her feminine, which is where she craves to be. While standing in your authentic strength, you are a champion and giving her that safe place to allow her to drop into her feminine self. Just hold her, let her sob, let her feel, let her vent. I know it sucks to be called a dumbass, asshole, or worse and not retort, but you can do it because you're a Remarkable Man.

Now look at her and hold her like you want to take her. Let her feel like your arms are the only place she wants to be. Here is where you become Remarkable in her eyes. She will slowly lose her anger and frustration. In fact, it's difficult to maintain the lower emotions when in this dynamic. You'll feel your power and she'll feel her femininity.

It is an effective transition of energy. Passion and sensuality is often the result.

This practice will take some courage, practice, and time, but the result is incredible. Remember—don't say a thing. Let your love for this woman come out in your actions, and hold space for her with authentic masculine energy. Through these actions, you're being Remarkable for everything that matters to you. Your wife, girlfriend, partner, or date longs to see and experience the Remarkable Man within you. Once she does, she will give you more in return than you ever thought possible.

We must start this process of being Remarkable, despite what women may think of us. The truth is the bar will be set high for all eternity. In fact, some women are in such pain they won't be happy until every man is removed from this earth. We are not to apologize or feel any less of a man because of the sins of our fathers and the men before them. Karma's a bitch and we all have to deal with our own. We are responsible for what we do in the here and now. Be the Remarkable Man you know you can be in this life. If that isn't good enough for the women in your life, it's time to spend time with women who will recognize and appreciate the champion you are.

We have but a finite amount of time on this planet. People come into our lives for a myriad of reasons, but love and romance are usually the most rewarding and joyous experiences we have. Put the women or partners you manifest in your life to share this incredible feeling in the Remarkable Man category of special care. Your fondest memories are usually about fun, closeness, and connection. She's in your life to give you that special feeling. Reward her and reward yourself...be her champion!

CHAPTER FIFTEEN

THE REMARKABLE MAN IN BUSINESS

Believe in yourself! Have faith in your abilities!
Without a humble but reasonable confidence in your own powers,
you cannot be successful or happy.
— Norman Vincent Peale

Your awareness of the way masculine and feminine energies play out will transcend your romantic relationships. This awareness can help you in your interactions with all people. These energies shift throughout your day, your week, and your life.

At work, how many times have you seen or witnessed someone passed over for a promotion, only to see a colleague with the same smarts and experience get the promotion? Maybe you know this someone *personally*? People can see if you're in your power or not. You can't fool anyone—at least not for long. Employers and clients want a person who's an inspiration. Status fits in nicely here too. When a man is in his authentic masculine power, he can rise to an inspiring level of power and responsibility. Both men and women shine in the business world when their masculine energy is cranked up.

One could argue that a woman's feminine power is what makes women successful. We could also argue that businesses are changing, or more accurately, evolving to a more feminine energy. This is a great step in the right direction, but we still have a way to go. The reality is that most businesses that are staffed by men have a predominantly masculine energy. Thus, the masculine energy serves you better in this dynamic to achieve success. I know many women who can balance their energy well and are superstars, no matter where they work.

Educated, business savvy, and attractive (by society's standards) women advance to leadership positions faster than do their male counterparts. Women just seem to have more drive than men. It could be they have something to prove, and kicking our asses in business is a good way to do it. Some people accuse women of using their feminine charm to get the sale or rise to the top. I'm sure a few women do that. You've probably met one or two. However, in most cases, the reason a woman got the sale or got to the top is because she was the total package—knowledgeable, attentive, and well put-together. Those who complain or gossip about her are usually jealous and find themselves left in her dust. Insecure, weak, and incompetent coworkers who can't stand being shown up create most of the rumors about superstar women.

A Remarkable Man is the total package for everyone he meets. Breathe deeply and on purpose, keep your shoulders back, and stand tall; always monitor your posture. When you open up your body size, it changes your energy and you feel more confident. Make your gestures and movements a tad slower, including blinking. Yes, blinking. Try it. Blink on purpose. There's something cool and calming about it. When you are fidgety and nervous, your movements are short, jerky, and tight. This body language screams, "I'm insecure and not very comfortable." This message makes others uneasy and reluctant to trust you.

Holding yourself with confidence works wonders when you walk into a crowded place to meet friends. Typically, you walk in and scan the place quickly and somewhat nervously to find those familiar faces in the crowd. If you want to be the guy with Remarkable presence, enter slowly, smile, and notice your surroundings. Notice the music, energy, and people. As you take in what you see, your friends may come into view naturally. However, YOU have come into view to other people, especially women. They'll see a man who isn't in a hurry. He moves with determination and is comfortable no matter where he is. A Remarkable Man has entered the room!

Be aware of your natural expression. I used to walk around thinking I was happy and feeling good. Then I'd see my reflection in a mirror or window. It shocked me! My expression was that of a very unhappy man! My natural facial expression, when my face was relaxed, was not very inviting. Try this test. Go to a mirror and totally relax your face. I'd venture to guess that your face doesn't express the energy you feel. A smile is rarely part of a relaxed face. It takes thirteen muscles to form a smile. Do some people-watching if you need proof. Most people walk around all day with sullen expressions on their faces. It doesn't necessarily mean they're unhappy; they might not be thinking about anything bad—they might just be on autopilot.

I looked into the mirror until I felt my natural expression. I imprinted how my muscles and skin felt when totally relaxed. Then I put on a more inviting and appealing expression—not a fake grin or expression of sheer happiness, but just an inviting, welcoming expression people would enjoy. Then I imprinted how my face felt, and how my muscles and skin moved to help form that expression. Now when I'm out in public, I'm much more aware of my facial expression.

Try this exercise. You'll be surprised by how much you stand out, how people are drawn to you. Practice a stronger physiology. Be cognizant of your posture at all times, both sitting and standing. Here's a biggie for many: holding eye contact while talking. Many people are uncomfortable with this practice. Try to hold eye contact for seven seconds or more without glancing away. It doesn't seem like much time, but if eye contact is outside your comfort zone, it might as well be forever! I challenge you to do it. When you're speaking with someone, hold his or her eye contact for seven seconds, then glance somewhere else for a second or two, and then back for seven seconds.

Then repeat. This behavior shows confidence, but it doesn't come across as freaky or intimidating. When you want to make a point, make solid, confident eye contact. When you listen, it's even more important to make eye contact. People need to feel you are fully engaged in what they are saying.

I could write a whole book about the subtleties of nonverbal communication, but you get the idea. The more you become a Remarkable Man, the more you will become aware of every aspect of your life and how you can interact more powerfully with others.

Success and The Remarkable Man. Success is easy, yet illusive. My life is a testament to that. If you desire success, it's there for you! The principles in this book, if applied, will help get you closer to your dream, your vision. What's *your* vision? I know you have one. The fact that you're reading this book tells me that your calling and vision have been gnawing at you for some time.

Many people have great ideas, but **action** leads to **results**, which lead to **abundance**. If your results are not what you want, then chances are you're not experiencing abundance, either. Knowing that, it's easy to deduce where your challenge is in this equation. It's your action (or lack thereof). How many of you are constantly building your vision? You know, spending time creating web sites, documents, articles, manuals, and all that social media that you just "have to" do? I learned the hard way that you can appear busy, and your action steps can be all about building your vision, but that's not what brings in the money.

Oh, we convince ourselves that creating all these "things" is necessary to bring in clients. However, there is time for that—and there's time for other activities. You want your day to be as productive as possible. By productive, I mean activity or action that puts cash into your bank account. It might mean picking up the phone and making that dreaded cold call. It could be an email blast to your database. Or it may be a follow up call to an existing client.

As you go about your day, ask yourself, "Is this a money-making activity? If it is, then postpone on all the back-end things you think you need to in order to build your business *after* you're finished with your money-making activities. Here are the three main areas that make you money. If you are not doing them, you are not making money:

1. Product Development

2. Marketing

3. Building Relationships

Make your time valuable by doing these activities during your set work time. Focus on constant growth. You cannot afford to sit back and relax on the successes of today. Each day should build on what happened the day before. Whether you're in business for yourself or work elsewhere, part-time or full-time, what you do during your workday will determine both your success and happiness within it.

I want to take this business chapter a step further. I developed this book to help men dig deep into their true passions. Your passion doesn't necessarily apply to a business goal. In fact, business could be the farthest thing from your vision. Who and what you are—right here, right now—is possibly a shell you want to shed. Maybe you want to find your inner rock star, mountaineer, or artist. It really does not matter what that calling is within you. What does matter is that you understand why you have this vision. Then ask yourself what you're going to do to make it happen. It's time to take action.

It's time to purchase that guitar, take a climbing lesson, or go to art school. It doesn't matter what you do, as long as you take an action step toward your goal. In the movie *The Bucket List*, both Jack Nicholas and Morgan Freeman's characters want to experience a few things they'd put off in their lives. With death upon them, they decide they must take action. Now, most of us don't have private jets and the means Jack Nicholas' character had to do all the things on their bucket lists. However, I wrote this book so that it won't take illness or impending death for you to realize just how fragile life can be.

What I challenge you to do is go to your "Champion's List" and pick just one item that resonates with you right now, one that's relatively inexpensive to accomplish and will give you the opportunity to feel great about crossing it off your list.

Now that you've made your selection, give yourself one week to put the wheels in motion. One week?! Yes, by putting a short timeframe on it, you create urgency and your brain and higher self will go to work on seeking ways to make it happen. Then show up and get it done! This little victory will give you the push you really need to get clear on your passions and dreams.

Show up for success in all you do. Focus on what makes you happy. Don't give into your fears. They aren't real. The unknown makes you hesitate. Neale Donald Walsch put fear into fantastic perspective. I'm sure you have heard various acronyms for the word "FEAR," but Walsch has an interesting spin that I have adopted.

FEAR—Feeling Excited And Ready. There is nothing to be afraid of. — Neale Donald Walsch

We've discussed the importance of understanding your place in the grand scheme of life—your life. The world is changing, and we're undergoing a dramatic shift in awareness and energy. As an individual, you're feeling that purpose, that passion, that inner knowing that shows up on a regular basis to help reinforce what you "should" be doing with your life.

You know, in the very depths of your soul, that things are not as they appear. You know you are meant to be, do, and have more. In other words, you can have it all...you really can. However, none of it will come your way until you start seeing yourself as a Remarkable Man. What you've experienced in life is a result of your past thinking. You see, the law of attraction is alive and well in you. Look at what you're attracting. Success is not all about business and how much stuff you have. How are your relationships with your family? I'm talking about your whole family, not just your wife and kids if you have them. How is your relationship with your parents? Perhaps they have passed on and you have wounds that did not heal before they left. Maybe you've been estranged from your sister or brother for something that should have been resolved years ago. Your outer success in this world is a small consolation if you are bankrupt in your mental, emotional, and spiritual world.

I can assess someone's inner world by how his outer world appears in his life. I'm good at this because I had myself as the greatest example. At times, I hated what showed up in my life. I hated myself. I hated God. I hated all things spiritual and esoteric because none of my dreaming and positive thinking manifested my destiny. I got quite the opposite: more debt, more lack, and more longing for a better life. How did I overcome the challenges, dramas, and frustrating story that made up my life?

I became a Remarkable Man. I became one because I decided to do so. I decided to end the drama. It occurred to me that I was getting back what I was giving. I'd complain and say that I worked hard and struggled, but it was all in vain because I faced more setbacks and drama. My story was that nothing ever worked for me. I was the victim. That's exactly what I'd share repeatedly—stories and dramas to justify, or even create, the crap I was living with.

Nothing outside you is your truth. Truth is subjective. You are not your job, your car, your house, your debt, your heartache, your addictions, your family, or any other label you give yourself. You are more, much more.

As I created this book, my life turned around. "The Remarkable Man" is about the truth, my truth. By writing and presenting it as a way to live my life, to guide my thoughts, decisions, and actions, I knew I could change dramatically.

That was the easy part: the thought of a book and the "what-if" power behind it. The challenge was actually completing it. Like so many other projects I'd embarked on, I wondered whether I was fooling myself. I'd always been a great starter and a poor finisher. Would this be another pipe dream, with me as a wannabe author? Well, the answer was right there. If I were going to write a book about being The Remarkable Man, I would have to stop thinking of myself as a poor finisher. I would have to change some of my deep beliefs in order to have success with such a grandiose undertaking.

Writing this book was indeed a challenge. However, I also had many moments of ease and grace when it seemed as though the words would never stop flowing. The challenges only came when I slipped back into lower thoughts and procrastinated about finishing, or when I allowed an old story to distort the truth of who I am.

However, as I got closer to completing this book, something magical began to happen in my life. I realized my choices were creating some great opportunities. The Remarkable Man was going to be more than a book; it was going to be a global brand and network for empowering men. Thus, The Remarkable Man Project ™ was born. This worldwide movement is here now to help champion men to be the best they can be. It's a brotherhood for celebrating the authentic masculine energy we all share. It's an invitation to join the first international men's group for creating Remarkable Men and bringing forth a new era of Remarkable leadership so we can create a Remarkable world.

CHAPTER SIXTEEN

BROTHERS TO EACH OTHER & SOME FINAL WORDS

My friend, we have a way to go if we are to show the world that men in general are not the ego-driven, power-hungry assholes many women and the media say we are. Nor are we the stupid, dufus, man-children portrayed on sitcoms and commercials. We do indeed have an uphill battle when it comes to cleaning up the image of men on this planet. Some politicians, generals, and warlords are not helping us out much. Religious fanatics and celebrity cheaters aren't assisting either.

But there's hope. A worldwide awakening of the authentic masculine power is taking place. With this awakening, men need to find one another and connect like never before. We must form a united front that enables us and supports us for who we really are...Remarkable Men.

There is no longer room for division. The dominating ego that caused this disconnection is gone. The old world of being alone on the journey is over, as we see the power in connection. We see the value in sharing our wisdom, gifts, and talents with our fellow Remarkable Men. We are all brothers, here to live, dream, and expand our possibilities. Each us has a key to helping a brother get where he needs to go.

Think of what can happen when men are empowered to live from their Remarkable Man selves. Then connect them with men throughout the world who are on the same path and energy vibration. These men want to get the most out of life. They want to embrace it, relish it, and celebrate it on their own terms.

The results can be epic. Imagine having Remarkable Men in every city and country. Imagine Remarkable Men influencing government and transnational corporations for a better tomorrow. Picture Remarkable Men helping their fallen brothers in prisons and in homeless shelters. Think about women talking about Remarkable Men with praise, admiration, and respect. Visualize children bragging about the Remarkable heroes in their lives.

Before any of this happens, we must first be brothers to each other. We must see ourselves as united and not as competition to be cheated, duped, or taken advantage of by each other. Remember, we are all here for a reason, a season, or a lifetime. Let's push each other to greatness rather than tear each other down. This idea is not a fantasy, but a reality in the making. I invite you to become a member of The Remarkable Man Project, the bold new face of leadership, empowerment, and networking. This project will result in a worldwide community of Remarkable Men being Remarkable in all they do. Within this project, you'll find your sanctuary, a "man cave" for your inner and outer growth, and all steps in between.

Imagine connecting with champions just like you from your own town and around the world for life-changing experiences and adventures. The Remarkable Man Project ™ is where you want to be. The goal is for one million Remarkable Men to join the movement to be Remarkable in all they are. Will one of them be *you*?

If you'd like to learn more about becoming a Remarkable Man (or if you're a woman who knows of a great guy who could benefit from these teachings), please visit **www.RemarkableManProject.com** to discover more about this incredible, life-changing project.

Being a Remarkable Man is not about just reading a book, pondering its message, and getting on with your life. The Remarkable Man is a movement in which you'll arrive, awake, and aware—if you take action. Through this book, I've presented a handful of sage advice and a few grains of wisdom. Please use this book as your catalyst for becoming Remarkable in your life. There has never been such a powerful pull toward your calling. You already know this, don't you? Your destiny is out there, begging you to put one foot in front of the other and just begin the journey.

Stop waiting for life to show up...it won't happen! You have to show up first. Dig deep within yourself and see the power, beauty, and passion that exists within you, my brother. Do not wait another day to be Remarkable in all you are.

It's time for you to be:

Champions to Women, Heroes to Children, and Brothers to Each Other.

I honor you, I believe in you, and I love you.

You are a Remarkable Man!

With Blessings and Gratitude...I've got your back!

Dwayne Klassen

ABOUT THE AUTHOR

Dwayne H. Klassen had what he calls his "perfect storm." In an 18 month period he lost his advertising company to less than honest partners, found out his 7 year old son was not his, and his new fiancé left him as a broken man. However, Dwayne's story is not one of tragedy but one of triumph. Dwayne used the adversity to create the most empowering chapter of his life and become a better man...a Remarkable Man.

Dwayne has been a serial entrepreneur, speaker, trainer and inventor for much of his adult life. Complete with both great wins and epic failures. But all perfectly executed to create the story of his life.

Dwayne is one of the top men's empowerment coaches.

He is the "The Mojo Coach" and the creator of The Remarkable Man Coaching Program - one of the most transformational and life changing processes a man will experience. It's the ultimate Remarkable Man incubator as he helps men dig deep into their authentic masculine power and ignite their identity, purpose and passion, so he can be the champion he longs to be.

Dwayne is also an entertaining and engaging international speaker on relationships, leadership, men's and women's issues and societal change. He is a visionary on how the masculine and feminine energy impacts all aspects of the human experience.

He is the Founder of The Remarkable Man Project - a global initiative to challenge one million men around the world to step up and play a bigger game. A membership based on-line community that provides men with the resources and support they need to become the Remarkable Man they know is within. Plus, it is an international brotherhood with RMP Chapters forming around the world. The world needs Remarkable Men!...Will you be one of them?

For more information on The Remarkable Man Coaching Program, workshops, press requests, or to book Dwayne Klassen to speak at your next event:

www.DwayneKlassen.com

Info@DwayneKlassen.com

For more information on The Remarkable Man Project visit:

www.RemarkableManProject.com

Join our communities on FaceBook:

www.facebook.com/DwayneHKlassenfanpage

www.facebook.com/RemarkableManProject

Follow Dwayne on Twitter:

twitter.com/Dwayneklassen

BONUS!

Join the **Remarkable Man Project** for a Free membership or sign up to be in Dwayne's Inner Circle and You'll Receive The RMP Weekly Newsletter.

PLUS!

Get Instant Access To Your Free Copy of Dwayne's Groundbreaking E-Book:

How To Create Your Remarkable Life

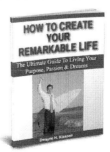

Made in the USA
Charleston, SC
22 March 2014